Front Cover Illustrati◌
Artist, Theodore Ge▪▪▪▪▪▪, ◌◌◌◌.
The Metropolitan Museum of Art.

Black History for Beginners:
The Myth of The Dangerous Black Man,
Jack Johnson, and The Great White Hope
© 2020 N.M. Shabazz. All Rights Reserved.
ISBN#9781648586408
Printed in the United States of America.
For more information: Blackhistoryforbeginners@gmail.com
Spoken History Education and Publishing Services
Kansas City, Missouri 64130

For bookclub information, please visit
www.facebook.com/historyforbeginners or e-mail
Blackhistoryforbeginners@gmail.com **to join our**
distribution list.

First Edition September 2020

Acknowledgement

This book is dedicated to Dr. Obidike Kamau.
While many have contributed to my education over the
years, when I met you, it was the first time that I could see
my own potential. Without you, I probably would not have
written any books. Yet, from day one on the campus
of Langston University—after I read your
Trippin' Back To Reality—new worlds opened.
I began to understand the voices in my head were not mere
bouts of insanity, but part of a talent yearning to escape. I
began to embrace myself as an *"artist"* and saw no shame in
the proclamation. You are the one who convinced me to
stop talking about it and *"be"* about it: Put pen to pad. My
prose is still not worthy of your glance, but I work to
compose a laudable exposition to make you proud. I will
always be the Padawan and you will always be
the wise, old, Jedi master.

Table of Contents

Additional Books in the Black History
for Beginners Series:

*Toussaint L'Ouverture, Napoleon Bonaparte,
and The Louisiana Purchase*

*The Great Migration, The Great Depression,
and Eleanor Roosevelt*

The Myth of The Dangerous Black Man, Jack Johnson, and The Great White Hope

D. Tyler Davis

Chapter One
The Myth of the Dangerous Black Man

"Concerning nonviolence, it is criminal to teach a man
not to defend himself when he is the constant victim of brutal attacks."
Malcolm X

In 2018, President Donald J. Trump granted a pardon to boxing legend Jack Johnson, the first African American Heavyweight Champion. Though the gesture was largely symbolic (Johnson died June 10, 1946), the irony of completing such an act was probably lost on the President who was not known for historical acumen. In part, Trump had signed the bill for political reasons (at the time, some of his own comments and actions bordered on racist) and also to one up his predecessor, President Barrack Obama (2008 – 2016, Democrat), an African American, whom he still appeared to compete with years after winning the Presidency.

But, why not pardon Johnson? The effort was token and cost Trump nothing. There were those, though, that saw things for what they truly were. Democratic political consultant Stefanie Brown James, remarked, *"...there are a lot of current, modern-day issues that he* [Trump] *could address as the living president that he chooses not to. I'm just personally tired of symbolism (Eligon & Shear, 2018)."* In June 1913, Johnson was convicted of a Federal crime for violation of the Mann Act (also known as the White Fugitive Slave Act), an obscure, draconian law that aimed to prevent the prostitution and degradation of women from immoral acts. In truth, however, Johnson had been convicted because of his intimate relationships with white women: Using the Mann Act was only the means to an end. His actual crime had been his audacity to believe the color line hadn't applied to him.

If Trump had known Johnson's full backstory, perhaps he would have hesitated or refused to even grant such a token legal remedy. Johnson is probably still in his casket, rolling around, cracking up over the President's stupidity. For much of his life, Johnson raised a middle finger to white America by refusing to lead his life according to their terms. He terrified the establishment by actually being the dangerous figure—the Baba Yaga—told to scare little boys and girls. Standing slightly over 6'0" and dark as midnight, he was perhaps more intimidating than Mike Tyson with a smile in the ring and just as gregarious and outspoken as Muhammad Ali outside of it. Yet, to fully comprehend America's abhorrence of Johnson, proper context needs to be established.

Though he was the fulfillment of the dark specter of arrogance America had so zealously been warning its daughters about for centuries, he only justified their beliefs that black men were, indeed, *"dangerous."* However, from where did this ideology originally come and was there any validity to it? To say the least, what would the likes of Trayvon Martin, Ahmaud Arbery, Botham Jean, and countless other men who were killed for simply being Black say to the belief? Is the statement that black men are dangerous a fact or a myth? While this query for some is highly debatable, for others it is a matter of perception.

Historically, black men have been characterized as hyperaggressive and hypersexual. In regard to the former, research by the American Psychological Association (APA) shows white men perceive black men as being bigger and more dangerous even when compared to other men of similar size. Foregoing the social implications this holds, the reality is that it produces above average murderous results. Black males die at a higher rate—2.5 times more—than their white counterparts when interacting with the police (Edwards, Esposito, & Lee, 2019); for black males aged 25 - 29 it is 2.8 – 4.1 times higher (Marshall, 2020). *"Unarmed black men are disproportionately more likely to be shot and killed by police, and often these killings are accompanied by explanations that cite the physical size of the person shot,' said lead author John Paul Wilson, PhD, of Montclair State University. 'Our research suggests that these descriptions may reflect stereotypes of black males that do not seem to comport with reality' (Wilson, 2017)."*

In his study, ***Racial Bias in Judgments of Physical Size and Formidability: From Size to Threat***, Wilson and others surveyed approximately 950 participants and showed them pictures of black and white men. They were of equal size, height, and weight. *"Participants also believed that black men were more capable of causing harm in a hypothetical altercation and, troublingly, that police would be more justified in using force to subdue them, even if the men were unarmed (Wilson, 2017)."*

This in itself should be enough to give one pause—the perception that one's race makes them more dangerous—but the incredulity doesn't stop there. As the old adage goes, *"The darker the berry, the sweeter the juice...,"* data shows it is even more perilous to be Black AND dark-skinned. *"While black men as a group face a particular threat of criminalization and disparate levels of lethal force when compared with white men, darker-skinned men are disproportionately targeted by the police.*

The majority of the high-profile cases involving police killings of black men bear out these finds. Case examples include Michael Brown (Missouri), Freddie Gray (Maryland), Walter Scott (Scott Carolina), Alton Sterling (Louisiana), Sam DuBose (Ohio), Philando Castile (Minnesota), and Corey Jones (Florida) (Davis, Stevenson, Western, Mauer, & Travis, 2018)." The study by Wilson and his colleagues echoed these sentiments. *"We found that men with darker skin and more stereotypically black facial features tended to be most likely to elicit biased size perceptions, even though they were actually no larger than men with lighter skin and less stereotypical facial features,'* said Wilson. *'Thus, the size bias doesn't rely just on a white versus black group boundary. It also varies within black men according to their facial features' (Wilson, 2017)."*

Interestingly enough, while black men appear larger than their white contemporaries, even when they are the same size, pictures of massive white men seem to have a more tantalizing effect. Colin Holbrook, a professor at UCLA, published a study, ***Evolution and Human Behavior***, that echoed similar findings to Wilson's, except with a sorted twist. *"Holbrook and his team found that when a white character was described as physically large, participants imagined him to be prestigious and respectable, commanding a room and owning it. But change one descriptor — add 'black' to the list of traits — and toss on a culturally stereotypical name* *and everything changes: Participants imagine someone potentially dangers, probably poor, maybe criminal (Basu, 2016)."*

Could this be the reason why black men—particularly young black men—die at a higher rate by the police than their white contemporaries? Because of cultural bias? It's befuddling that two people—both of the human race—can elicit such profound differences in perception and expectation. Notwithstanding the police, what does this mean for Blacks—especially if they are large or darker skinned—in corporate America or in elementary or secondary schools? Surely, the police can't be the only ones who are failing black men. Regarding schools in the United States:

- *The school suspension rate for African Americans is three times more than white students; out of school suspensions are given out to 20% of black male students versus 6% of white male students*
- *Pre-school African Americans are also three times more likely to be sent home for transgressions than white preschoolers*
- *In 2011, approximately 20% of Oakland's African America students were kicked out of school at least once, which was six times more than white students*
- *For the 2009 – 2010 school year in Chicago, though black students comprised 45% of the student body in the city's public schools, they accounted for 76% of its suspensions (Taylor, Guy, & Wilke, 2019)*

Given the above, one would think there would be some sort of national outcry or effort to change this *"dangerous"* perception. Yet, black males' demonized mythos is too firmly rooted in the fabric and culture of American history to vanish easily, particularly when society exacerbates the myth so wantonly. Popular media most often displays black men as aggressors, even if that aggression is played out subtly through sports (thus, the lore that Blacks are physically better at most sports; i.e. basketball, football, and boxing).

This only helps to reinforces the *"dangerous"* myth. *"Men of color held in esteem by the media, while entirely worthy of praise, too often personify a circumscribed spectrum of human qualities. Prowess in sports, physical achievement in general and musicality are emphasized inordinately. Common role models depicted by the media such as rap or hip-hop stars and basketball players imply limited life choices. When is the last time you have seen a black college professor, doctor, lawyer or scientist selling a product? Many important dynamics that affect black lives, such as history of economic disadvantage and a prevailing anti-black bias in society, don't often make it to the presses or the screens (Donaldson, 2015)."*

Then, there are the detractors—legislators and politicians—who protect the fallacy. In July 2020, when questioned about the rate of black deaths by the hands of law enforcement and why so many black men were dying because of them, even the President dismissed the issue by retorting, *"So are white people. So are white people. What a terrible question to ask. So are white people,' Trump told* **CBS News** *in an interview on Tuesday. 'More white people, by the way. More white people' (Thomsen, 2020)."*

According to Matt Miller, a professor at Northeastern University, people like Trump who make statements like this are being disingenuous at best. In a Northeastern - Harvard study, he found that, though Blacks only make up 12% of the United States population, they made up 25% of the deaths in police related shootings. Furthermore, *"In those instances where the victims appear to pose a minimal-or-less threat to police, based on the data we had, Black people were three times as likely to be killed," Miller says. "That doesn't mean the police didn't feel threatened. But based on the reports that we were able to look at, a very low level of threat was directed at the police. And in those specific cases, the numbers rose for Black people: They made up 36 percent of the deaths (Thomsen, 2020)."*

In refuting the President, he goes on to state, *"Trump's lack of curiosity about why this is happening is indicative of not really caring about getting to the bottom of the problem. You can't solve a problem unless you know what the problem is in the first place (Thomsen, 2020)."* To be fair, Trump isn't the only one who doesn't want to get to the bottom of the problem. Much of white America has trepidation when facing the realities of its present and past because all roads lead to slavery. This forever appears to be a prohibited topic: It forces the mainstream to deal with its legacy of guilt. However, until America adequately discusses slavery—its ramifications and racism in proper context—this problem will continue to adversely affect black males in the foreseeable future. Speaking of slavery…

"Stereotypes about African-Americans in the USA are products of the institution of slavery. These deeply held beliefs stem from White racist attitudes that were operationalized through oppressive and discriminating actions that idealized how slaves should think and behave (Taylor, Guy, & Wilke, 2019)." Stereotypes about Blacks were created to justify their subjugation and exploitation through political, social, and economic means. It is easier to stereotype a race if it does not look like the mainstream society or does not share a common history. Of course, Black and Whites DO share a common history, but unfortunately most of that history starts at the beginning of the Transatlantic Slave Trade: A shared history wherein Blacks started off as the captured and Whites the capturers.

During slavery, black men were stereotyped into two groups, the Sambo and the Brute (Green, n.d.). Sambos (also labelled as Coons, with minor differences) were known for their compliance and stupidity, Brutes for their physical strength and proclivities towards mindless violence and rebellion. Both of these stereotypes served justifiable purposes. While Sambos did work (if prodded), they were renowned for being shiftless and lazy.

Blacks were supposed to be an intellectually inferior and incompetent race. In fact, Whites *"saved"* them from the harsh, savage jungles of Africa (as if they didn't already have thriving kingdoms and culture during this time). Sambos needed white slavers for direction for, if slavers were not around, they might all starve. This justified slavery, transforming the slave master from an oppressor into a saint. *"The supporters of slavery claimed that blacks were a childlike people unequipped for freedom. Proslavers acknowledged that some slave masters were cruel, but they argued that most were benevolent, kind-hearted capitalists who civilized and improved their docile black wards (The Coon Caricature, n.d.)."*

The following compares a Sambo and a Coon:

"The coon caricature is one of the most insulting of all anti-black caricatures. The name itself, an abbreviation of raccoon, is dehumanizing. As with Sambo, the coon was portrayed as a lazy, easily frightened, chronically idle, inarticulate, buffoon. The coon differed from the Sambo in subtle but important ways. Sambo was depicted as a perpetual child, not capable of living as an independent adult. The coon acted childish, but he was an adult; albeit a good-for-little adult. Sambo was portrayed as a loyal and contented servant. Indeed, Sambo was offered as a defense for slavery and segregation. How bad could these institutions have been, asked the racialists, if blacks were contented, even happy, being servants? The coon, although he often worked as a servant, was not happy with his status. He was, simply, too lazy or too cynical to attempt to change his lowly position. Also, by the 1900s, Sambo was identified with older, docile blacks who accepted Jim Crow laws and etiquette; whereas coons were increasingly identified with young, urban blacks who disrespected whites. Stated differently, the coon was a Sambo gone bad (The Coon Caricature, n.d.)."

In newspapers, Sambos were drawn as having dark skin and full, exaggerated lips that protruded from the mouth like small dinner plates. They were highly illiterate and often talked with broken English: *"I'se be catchin' ma feets nah, Boss (The Coon Caricature, n.d.)."*

It is important to note the image of the Sambo was heavily promoted BEFORE the Civil War—when slavery was allowed—and the image of the Brute heavily promoted AFTER it ended. *"These portrayals were pragmatic and instrumental. Proponents of slavery created and promoted images of blacks that justified slavery and soothed white consciences. If slaves were childlike, for example, then a paternalistic institution where masters acted as quasi-parents to their slaves was [sic] humane, even morally right. More importantly, slaves were rarely depicted as brutes because that portrayal might have become a self-fulfilling prophecy (Pilgrim, 2012)."*

In other words, the South did not want to spread propaganda about Brutes because it might give slaves ideas about rebellion, freedom, and—Lord forbid—being with a white woman. Of course, after the Civil War, it was a different story. Propaganda was needed to help keep the black man intimidated. If fear about him could be effectively disseminated to the mainstream, the social pressure would keep him in line, even if this *"pressure"* was sometimes distributed via lynchings, race riots, or through terrorist groups like the Ku Klux Klan (KKK).

The Brute (also known as the Savage), was a strong, mindless barbarian who, left to his own machinations, would destroy and consume all of those around him. In as much as the Brute was prized for his strength and endurance, he was equally feared and hated for his supposed insatiable lust for white women. A key example of the Brute or Savage are the white actors in black face, chasing *"chaste"* white women, in D.W. Griffin's racist 1915 movie, **"Birth of a Nation,"** which was the first movie ever to be ever shown in the White House.

"The premiere of 'Birth of a Nation' during the reconstruction period in 1915 marked the change in emphasis from the happy Sambo and the pretentious and inept Jim Crow stereotypes to that of the Savage. In this D.W. Griffith film, the Ku Klux Klan tames the terrifying, savage African-American through lynching. Following emancipation, the image of the threatening brute from the 'Dark Continent' was revitalized (Basu, 2016)."

Saving the fairer sex from the Brute during slavery became a reoccurring theme. The effort particularly intensified after the Civil War (it was white American's belief that every black man secretly harbored an intimate affinity toward white women), because now the Brute was free to do as he wished: No longer constrained, his natural, animalistic tendencies would lead him down the path to pillaging and raping white women. He was too much of a *"savage"* and couldn't help himself. Thus, the stereotype of the Brute was mainstream society's way of protecting their females from him by any means necessary.

"As Sally Kitch explains in her book **The Specter of Sex: Gendered Foundations of Racial Formation in the United States,** *'[V]iolence against men of color usually entailed explicit or implicit suspicions of sexual aggression, perversion, or intention; and implications that all competition between men of color and white men – over land or horses or sex – somehow threatened white manhood and white women's virtue' (Loubriel, 2016)."*

A live action illustration of a Brute is in Richard Fleischer's controversial 1975 movie, *"Mandingo,"* starring James Mason, Susan George, Perry King, Richard Ward, Brenda Sykes, and boxer-turned actor Ken Norton. Set in the Deep South prior to the Civil War, Mede (Ken Norton) is a Mandingo slave purchased by Hammond (Perry King). Hammond is in awe of Mede's physical makeup and strength. Soon, he places Mede in a series of fights against slaves from other plantations. The more brutal the contests (they could hardly be called boxing matches; the fights were outright, last-man standing, MMA-like brawls) the more exhilarating they were to the myriad slave owners and other Whites gathered to watch and place bets on the big, black *"bucks."*

In a particularly wrenching scene, Mede kills an opponent by taking a chomp out of his jugular vein. As he engages in more contests, Mede's fighting skills develop and he wins Hammond lots of money, which raises Mede's profile on the plantation. In no time, he is offered his pick of female slaves as reward from which to breed (the one exception being a slave for which Hammond has affections). Shown favor by his slave master, Mede's life is a relaxed one. He arrogantly takes for granted Hammond's positive outlook toward him.

He also thinks he is above the other slaves on the plantation, although one slave—a literate, secretly rebellious male named Agamemnon (Richard Ward)—tries to get Mede to stay in his lane. *"When are you going to learn the color of your skin, Mede?"* he asks the Mandingo, who is sitting on the ground, out of breath from a training session Hammond had just finished supervising. Taking his time, gathering himself, Mede replies sarcastically, *"Just as soon as you stop puttin' on you smilin' nigger face…for Massa Hammond!"*

The climax of the film comes as Hammond's newly estranged wife, Blanche (Susan George) becomes despondent and resentful that her husband would rather receive his intimate pleasures from female slaves than from her. Discovering that a slave (Brenda Sykes) is pregnant with Hammond's child, Blanche goes exceptionally medieval in her actions when her husband leaves for a business excursion. She beats the slave so severely that the slave loses the baby.

In a different scene, Blanche's curiosity implores her to discover what makes Mede so *"special."* Seeking revenge of sorts on her husband, and finding the male slave aesthetically scrumptious, Blanche forces Mede to have sex. When he at first refuses her advances, she threatens to tell everyone that he raped her. Faced with an *"I'm damned if I do, damned if I don't"* moment, he reluctantly has intercourse with her…several times.

Later, when Blanche becomes pregnant, Hammond— thinking the gestating child is his—beams with pride; this is, until a baby mulatto exits the womb and it's obvious the child is not. The next scenes involve a frenetic pace of emotion. The doctor *"mercifully"* orders the child to be killed. Consequently, for his wife to have had sex with a black man is a transgression Hammond simply cannot forgive. He murders Blanche by giving her poison used to dispatch old slaves and horses, putting it in a toddy that he gives her to drink.

Once she is dead, Hammond then turns his full rage onto Mede, whom he orders to, *"…fill a big kettle of water and strike a fire under it."* Questioning his master's intentions and sensing his impending doom, Mede nonetheless does as he is asked. Later, when the cauldron of water is bubbling from the massive fire raging underneath, he directs Mede to get in it. Pleading for his life, Mede protests and tells his master of Blanche's threat to blackmail him into having sex with her, but to no avail. Hammond's mind is made up.

Regardless whether or not his prized slave is telling the truth, he still has to kill him. What would happen if word got out and people learned he had allowed Mede to live? He would be a disgrace and would be forced to live in shame. Hammond shoots Mede with a rifle, knocking him into the boiling cauldron. Writhing in pain, Mede struggles to get out until Hammond discards the rifle and picks up a pitchfork to pin Mede down in the water.

The movie ends when Agamemnon picks up the weapon, shoots Hammond's father, Warren (James Mason), and then flees the scene. Though it did relatively well at the box office, the film was immediately deadpanned by the movie elite in Hollywood. Among these was famed movie critic Robert Ebert who gave it a harsh diatribe, rating it with zero stars (Ebert, 1975). *"Mandingo' is racist trash, obscene in its manipulation of human beings and feelings, and excruciating to sit through in an audience made up largely of children, as I did last Saturday afternoon. The film has an 'R' rating, which didn't keep many kids out, since most came with their parents (Ebert, 1975)."* In his review, Ebert rails against kids being in the movie and how inappropriate it was for them to view it.

However, what's more astonishing is how **"Mandingo"** appears to have elicited such visceral emotions in him, as it did in many white critics who had a low opinion of the movie. Zero stars? Although it was no **"Roots"** by Alex Haley, **"Mandingo"** did feature an A-list cast with a decent script and acting. Many thought they were going to a movie to view slavery through the eyes of slaves. Instead, they saw it through the eyes of the oppressor—depicting them as monsters and lusty fools. Could this have been the reason why the movie was so widely disdained?

Despite its rawness and extreme situations, it speaks to the reality many slaves faced. For reference, all one has to do is look at the many black descendants Thomas Jefferson had with his *"favorite"* slave Sally Hemmings, or the numerous other *"lovechild"* mulattos sprung from slave masters' late night excursions to slave quarters. This part is not Hollywood fiction, but documented fact. Ebert should not have been so stuck in his feelings. The movie speaks not to an exact history of slavery (even though, historically, many things covered did happen to slaves), but more to the fear and paranoia that white men had of black men.

"Mandingo," the Brute or Savage, was their worst nightmare come true. *"Headlines of newspapers across the nation, beginning around the turn-of-the-century, document a frenzy of arrests,* *attempted lynchings and murders of 'black brutes' accused of insulting or assaulting white women. Heavyweight boxing champion Jack Johnson epitomized the Mandingo or Black Brute of white imaginations in the flesh. Called a beast, a brute and a coon in print, Johnson's relationships with white women took up as much newsprint as his fighting abilities (Popular and Pervasive Stereotypes of African Americans, n.d.)."*

Even pseudo-science tried to justify the oppression of Blacks by claiming they were biologically inferior to Whites. In making his hierarchical pyramid of the five races, Johann Friedrich Blumenbach, a German scientific *"classifier"* of the 18th century and the person who created the term Caucasian in 1795, placed Whites at the top. Of course, this model of scientific nonsense was embraced by much of the world at the time and continued be into the early part of the 20th century. Later, in 1781, Thomas Jefferson would publish his **Notes on the State of Virginia**.

Apparently, although his female slaves were fine to have sexual intercourse with, Jefferson did not believe that Blacks were intellectually or culturally equal to Whites, either. Here are several excerpts (Jefferson, n.d.):

> *"I advance it therefore, as a suspicion only, that blacks...are inferior to whites in the endowments of body and mind."*

> *"In general, their existence appears to participate more of sensation than reflection. In my imagination, they are dull [and] tasteless...This unfortunate difference of colour, and perhaps of faculty, is a powerful obstacle to the emancipation of these people."*

> *"Deep rooted prejudices...real distinctions which nature has made...and many other circumstances will probably never end but in the extermination of the one or the other race."*

Hold up. What was Jefferson REALLY talking about when he wrote, *"...real distinctions which nature has made..."*? It should be obvious, since Blacks were toward the bottom of the hierarchical pyramid. Ibram X. Kendi, a professor at American University in Washington, states of Jefferson's **Notes on the State of Virginia**, *"This was one of the...best-selling nonfiction books in early America,"* he said. *"And black and other* *anti-racist activists were arguing against Jefferson's theory of black intellectual inferiority into the 1830's (Ruane, 2019)."*

Next in 1839 enters Samuel Morton, an American scientist, whose partial claim to fame was that he had *"proved"* black mental inferiority by declaring that their skulls were smaller than Whites. Of course, since they had smaller skulls, this meant Whites had cognitive advantage over Blacks. *"Their larger skulls give Caucasians decided and unquestioned superiority over all the nations of the earth."* (Morton's findings were widely embraced, despite *"...systemic errors in favor of his assumptions... (Race, the Power of Illusion: Go Deeper Timeline, n.d.)"*

As if this wasn't ludicrous enough, on March 17, 1851, a *"scientist,"* Samuel Cartwright, delivered a paper in Louisiana, **A Report on the Diseases and Physical Peculiarities of the Negro Race**, that told of the reason why some slaves would suddenly get rebellious, want freedom, and stage an uprising. This *"disease"* had a name; Drapetomania, which was a mental paralysis or debasement of the mind that overcame slaves and made them want to seek freedom.

"In noticing a disease not heretofore classed among the long list of maladies that man is subject to, it was necessary to have a new term to express it. The cause in the most of cases, that induces the negro to run away from service, is as much a disease of the mind as any other species of mental alienation, and much more curable, as a general rule. With the advantages of proper medical advice, strictly followed, this troublesome practice that many negroes have of running away, can be almost entirely prevented, although the slaves be located on the borders of a free state, within a stone's throw of the abolitionists (Cartwright, n.d.)."

Cartwright even went as far as to claim that blood vessels in black brains were smaller than white brains and that this sometimes contributed to their madness. He used shoddy *"science"* and misinterpreted bible verses to support his position. Yet, this didn't stop him from making a declarative claim. *"The membranes, the muscles, the tendons...even the negro's brain and nerves...are tinctured with a shade of pervading darkness (Ruane, 2019)."* The fact that Cartwright was friends with Jefferson Davis, future president of the Confederacy, did not bode well for the black man down South. He was later appointed to a professorship at what is now Tulane University.

Ironically, Cartwright's thinking would be echoed over 150 years later by Dylann Roof, the white supremacist and mass murderer who killed nine people—all Black—on June 17, 2015, at the Emanuel African Methodist Episcopal Church. Earlier during that year on social media, Roof had posted a manifesto stating, *"Negroes have lower Iqs [sic], lower impulse control, and higher testosterone levels in generals [sic]. These three things alone are a recipe for violent behavior (Ruane, 2019)."*

In 1859, Charles Darwin published **On the Origin of Species**, which discussed the theory of evolution. Though Darwin never meant for his research to be applied to humans, in 1864, after reading his work, an English philosopher, Herbert Spenser, coined the phrase *"survival of the fittest"*. This led to the concept of Social Darwinism: That the lives of humans in society are a struggle for existence ruled by *"survival of the fittest."* This meant that the weak, or those who were on the bottom of the social ladder, were in their situation because nature made them that way or because they were pre-destined to be that way.

Social Darwinism soon became another way to justify the oppression of Blacks and other people of color. Later in the 19th century, it also became another justification for the Robber Barons in the United States—such as Cyrus Field, Jay Gould, Cornelius Vanderbilt, and others—to continue to use unscrupulous means to get rich or expand their wealth. In 1883, there came the birth of eugenics, which means *"good genes."* Francis Galton, Darwin's cousin, invented the term.

"During the Progressive era (1900-1920), a generation of American reformers sought to fix several social problems of the day, which included urban poverty, assimilating the huge number of immigrants coming to American shores, and public health crises such as epidemics, high infant mortality rates and explosive population growth. Many of these reformers used inappropriate eugenic explanations for their management of those deemed to be socially undesirable: so-called 'mental defectives' (which

included those labeled with newly-created clinical terms like 'imbeciles,' 'idiots,' and 'morons'); the blind, deaf, mentally ill and 'crippled'; orphans, unwed mothers, epileptics, Native Americans, African Americans, foreigners, poor residents from the mountains and hollows of Appalachia and many other 'outsider' groups (Markel, 2018)." (To be fair, W.E.B. DuBois' *"Talented Tenth"* concept is a form of eugenics; Hitler's *"master race"* and his genocide of Jews during World War II is a blatant form of eugenics). Understanding the zeitgeist and the perspective of Blacks by Whites before Jack Johnson's rise in boxing is imperative for one to overstand the significance of everything he accomplished.

Tall and black as midnight, with a strong build and a determined mind, he was both the Brute and the Sambo about which white America had long warned everyone. Physically gifted? Yes. Inherently dumb? Not even in the slightest. Always dressed cleaner than a Kansas City pimp, with impunity he openly pursued, courted, and seduced some of the most beautiful white women of his era: Actresses Mae West and Lupe Velez; German spy Mata Hari; and French actress and singer Mistinguett (Weinreb, 2016).

He was not only the first black man to win the Heavyweight title, he was one of the first black men to blatantly, arrogantly challenge the system of racism in the United States head on, with virtually no allies or political help. Johnson was always most comfortable in the ring, where he could dictate things and control his own destiny. Perhaps, then, it is with a certain poetic frustration that the only things he seemingly couldn't control was his life outside of it.

Chapter Two
Jack Johnson

"I made a lot of mistakes out of the ring, but I never made any in it."
Jack Johnson

There is underlying irony President Trump was motivated to pardon Johnson. In many ways, the two were cut from the same cloth. On numerous occasions, pundits have labelled Trump as a narcissist—his lack of empathy, the ability to make every situation about him—and Johnson displayed signs of the trait throughout adulthood. Though many falsehoods have been created about him, sorting out Johnson's larger than life mythos is somewhat disheartening.

In the 1960's, black radicals and white liberals remade his image into a man who was dogged by the power structure simply because he chose to marry a white woman and refused to bow down to white men. While much of this is true, there is a lot which is not. Johnson did not antagonize the white power structure in America to strike a blow for the black man. He did what he did because he was Jack Johnson. The impudence of challenging Social Darwinism or Jim Crow was lost on him, except when it served his purposes.

As Randy Roberts states in his book, ***Papa Jack: Jack Johnson and the Era of White Hopes***, *"The real Jack Johnson was not a stereotype. Nor was he the black hero that young black radicals of the 1960s were looking for. He was not the ghost in the house, as poetic Bundi Brown told Ali. Where Ali was proudly black and political, Johnson's racial attitude was much more confused. His hatred of the white world was almost as deep as his longing to be part of it. Although he was admired by thousands of blacks during his own day, he refused the responsibility of leadership, and he could not lead by example for to follow his example was to court disaster. On only one point was Johnson consistent throughout his life: he accepted no limitations. He saw no inconsistency in ridiculing a white boxer in the ring and then celebrating with white friends. And if his conquest of white women was in part a desire to humiliate the white race, it was because he preferred white women to black women. He was not a simple man. Johnson's* *greatest strength was also his most glaring weakness. His life was the result of a supreme ego (Roberts 1983)."* To put it succinctly, Johnson was an arsehole.

John Arthur Johnson was born on March 31, 1878, in Galveston, Texas, the third son of nine children (three of whom died in child birth), to Henry and Tina Johnson. Both parents had been former slaves and were of modest means (this is putting things lightly; they were dirt poor). Allegedly, Johnson's father, born in Maryland in 1838, had been a bare-knuckle boxer who had fought to entertain wealthy white plantation owners (Roberts,1983). Illiterate, in poor health, and suffering from a gimp leg, Henry Johnson was nonetheless a proud, hardworking laborer, eventually becoming a janitor at a school.

He married Tina, 19 years younger than he, who worked as a domestic servant. Though the two didn't have much, in the 1880's they managed to buy a plot of land in Galveston, total value $400, on which they built a house, probably of the *"shotgun"* variety. Still, for Henry, it was an accomplishment. *"Henry's holdings were meager even in a poorer section in Galveston. But he did own the land and house outright, and for an ex-slave this in itself was a proud accomplishment (Roberts, 1983)."* By 1900, the house Henry had built was worth $500 and the land $600.

The couple later lost everything on September 7 of that year in the *"Great Storm"* that swept through the area (the *"Great Storm"* was one of the deadliest hurricanes in U.S. history, leaving over 6,000 dead and $15,000,000 in property damage, the equivalent of $462,680,000 in today's money). Henry and Tina, pious people, had to start over from scratch to rebuild what had taken a lifetime to amass. Jack grew up in Galveston's decrepit 12th Ward, a place so run down he claimed that the white people who lived there among the Blacks were too poor to be racist.

In fact, one of the reasons he later acted with such insolence toward white men was because he had never grown up fearing them. As a little boy, white children were among his friends. Johnson had developed comradery with them and had been close to their parents. *"As I grew up, the white boys were my friends and my pals. I ate with them, played with them and slept at their homes. Their mothers gave me cookies, and I ate at their tables. No one ever taught me that white men were superior to me (Ward, 2004)."* He would not experience racism until he later left home and explored life outside his bubble.

Henry and Tina Johnson, Methodists, made sure all of their children went to church and were educated, although education during this time was somewhat subjective. Jack attended five years of elementary school. He was never supposed to be an intellectual or a white-collar worker, but a laborer just like his father and five years of schooling was all one needed. Though Johnson quit school to find a job to help the family, the future he saw for himself was one away from Galveston's ghettos, despite not fully realizing how he would make his escape. He never kept a job long, but eventually ended up working at the docks. By then, wander lust had started to develop…along with an affinity for boxing.

Already drawn to the sport, while traveling around looking for employment during this time, Johnson began to discover his inner self; that he was different from most boys his age. His stamina and strength were above average. *"Johnson's real education came about during endless hours of drifting about Galveston and south Texas. He learned that he was physically superior to other youths, that he was quicker and could punch harder (Roberts, 1983)."* Johnson's mother, Tina, is credited as being the first pugilistic influence in his life.

Rumor has it that as a little boy Johnson was cowardly, with his sister Lucy taking up for him in fights on the schoolyard. One day, his mother told him that if he came back crying again, complaining about being bullied, she was going to really give him something to cry about. That day, the legend of Jack Johnson—the *"Galveston Giant"*—was born. Perhaps the most amazing thing about him is that he was never formally trained in the art of boxing. Most of the losses on his record (95 Total Fights; 70 Wins; 35 Knockouts; 11 Loses; 11 Draws; 3 No Contests) come either from his early days of fighting, or in the mid 1920's when he was way past his prime.

As a young teenager, his pugilistic education came in the form of the Battle Royal (sometimes spelled with an *"e"* on the end). Despite the concept of the Battle Royal (a duel or fight between two or more people at the same time) existing for thousands of years, in America it has a particularly racist overtone. During slavery, groups of black men would be thrown into makeshift rings and ordered to fight for the amusement of plantation owners and other whites (Bressin, n.d.). The last man standing won and was usually granted some form of reward, although the cash prize was seldom his to keep. (Ralph Ellison gives a vivid account of a Battle Royal in his epic novel, **Invisible Man**).

"Formerly enslaved with about seventy-five others on a cotton plantation in Jackson County, Alabama, John Finnely recalled one of the few amusements he and his fellow slaves shared in their days of bondage. For 'joyments,' remembered Finnely, 'weuns have de co'n huskin an' de nigger fights.' Finnely delighted in his recollection of the slave fights he witnessed growing up in antebellum Alabama, noting that although the fights were 'mo' fo' de w'ite fo'k's 'joyment,' the slaves were also 'lowed to see it.' According to Finnely, the masters of different plantations matched their slaves by size and then bet on them (Lussana, 2010)."

Roberts (1983) adds, *"This form of boxing contest was more ritual than sport; it served to debase black youths before the white enforcers of the Southern racial system. Battle Royals had only one theme but a number of variations. The single theme involved black youth fighting in front of white spectators, who threw pennies and nickels to the victor. The lesson was obvious: rewards came from defeating your brother, not from joining him. Only rarely did a Battle Royal entail a single man-on-man confrontation. Usually, eight or mor black youths were told to get into the ring and fight a free-for-all. No rules were observed, and only the last person standing won any money (Roberts,1983)."*

Boxing matches between slaves were also a way plantation owners kept their wards' minds busy so they wouldn't plot a rebellion against them (Gilmore, *Black Athletes In An Historical*

Context: The Issue of Race, 1995). Al-Tony Gilmore (1995) discusses the blacks' role in boxing during slavery. *"With the handsome earnings that a talented slave boxer could make for his owner coupled with the popularity and frequency of pugilistic competition among slaves, boxing became the primary occupation—work assignment for such slaves. Nonetheless, the brutal and primitive nature of slave boxing classified it as a risky line of work only to be pursued by the brave, bold and physically gifted. Repeated failure as a slave boxer often resulted in demotion from athletic status to reassignment to the more conventional slave worker responsibilities."*

Though he had participated in street and dock fights, the Battle Royal would be the first type of *"organized"* boxing in which Johnson would engage. Increasingly, he came to be the last man standing. Sometimes in such contests, his foes would join forces in an effort to dispatch him. Increasingly, they failed. One by one, Johnson would back them into a corner, talk smack (imagine him playing *"The Dozens"* simultaneously while fighting), and then give them a walloping as if they had stolen from the church. By 18 years old, most of his time was dedicated to boxing and he was earning more in one night fighting than his father would earn all week (Barnes P. , Burns, & Schaye, 2004). Johnson's boxing education in his late teens was later furthered when he became a sparring partner for other pugilists.

By age 20, he had turned professional and travelled the country, hitchhiking on trains like a hobo if needed. During the era in which Johnson started fighting, boxing in America had an infamous reputation and was not seen as *"honorable."* Somewhat distinguished in England, Americans looked at the sport as sordid, full of corruption, and favored mostly by the lower class. To many, the fights were no more than displays in barbarism. There was no such thing as a boxing commission (champions were frequently *"crowned"* by public sentiment) and rarely were there ever any ringside doctors.

While the upper crust did support boxing as an athletic endeavor, that was about the extent of it. Even President Theodore Roosevelt (March 4, 1901 – March 4, 1909,

Republican) was one of those who was staunchly against prizefighting, despite having participated on Harvard University's boxing team in college. For some reason, he later developed a particular abhorrence to it after Johnson won the Heavyweight title (Franco, 2016).

Boxing historian Burt Sugar (2004) says that in Johnson's day the three biggest sports in America were Horseracing, Baseball, and Boxing: The latter was a fringe sport that had yet to earn the full respect of the nation (Barnes P. , Burns, & Schaye, 2004). The man who made sport reverent for public consumption in America was Heavyweight Champion John L. Sullivan (Sullivan was Heavyweight Champion from 1882 – 1892). Consequently, though Sullivan brought some form of respectability; there was one thing neither he nor most white fighters would ever dare do to disrespect it: Cross the color line.

As a general rule, white boxers fighting black boxers was discouraged, especially in the heavyweight ranks. The only exceptions to this were if a white boxer was washed up, had a mediocre record, really needed the money, or was simply going to be a journeyman for most of his career. For those just starting out or showing promise, the risk of losing to a black boxer was too great a threat to their reputations. *"Loyal Southerner"* Henry Long, interviewed by the **New Orleans Daily Picayune**, echoed these sentiments.

"The idea of niggers fighting white men. Why, if that darned scoundrel would beat that white boy the niggers would never stop gloating over it, and, as it is, we have enough trouble with them (Sommers, 1966)." **Jack Johnson versus Jim Crow: Race, Reputation, and the Politics of Black Villainy: The Fight of the Century** tells us, *"…it is important to note that the boxing ring of the late 19th and early 20th centuries was, in many respects, a microcosm of US society. Championship fights were, for the most part, all-white affairs and the segregated boxing ring mirrored America's preoccupation with keeping African Americans 'in their place' and on the outside of the US racial hierarchy (Alderman, Inwood, & Tyner, 2018)."*

George Dixon—a Canadian—became the first black champion of any sport in 1890 when he won the Bantamweight title by knocking out Englishman Nunc Wallace (George Dixon, 2020). However, part of the reason Dixon was able to win the title was because he was Canadian and had fought Wallace on English soil. If Dixon had been a black American fighting a white American boxer, the fight probably never would have happened. Puffing his chest out to fellow pugilists in 1892, Sullivan expressly said, *"In this challenge I include all fighters—first come, first served—who are white. I will not fight a Negro; never have and never shall (Roberts, 1983)."*

Texas had outlawed boxing in 1889; contests could only take place if a $500 levy (the equivalent of $14,081.00 in today's money) was posted. In 1891, the state outright prohibited prizefighting (Roberts, 1983). Any fight between men for sport was a punishable felony that came with a fine (between $500 – $1,000) and/or, possible jail terms ranging from 60 days up to one year. While this did not stop prizefighting in Texas, it did slow it down. There were always going to be those who sought a way around the law, though. Sugar (2004) says that in some states where boxing was prohibited, promoters would sometimes hold fights on barges or in farmers' fields to keep lawmen away (Barnes P. , Burns, & Schaye, 2004).

In 1880, Sullivan had done such a thing—fighting and beating John Flood in eight rounds—while on a barge floating in the Hudson River to avoid authorities (Roberts & Skutt, 2006). In 1889, the Galveston Athletic Club bid Joe Choynski, a boxer who had obtained some national renown, to be the organization's training instructor. After the club agreed to a $500 a month stipend, his first *"scientific demonstration"* was to be against Jim Hall, a local heavyweight journeyman. On February 25, 1901, Choynski—whose skills, by then, were fading—knocked Johnson out in the third round. (Johnson had returned to Galveston specifically to fight Choynski). As the referee was finishing the count, Captain Brooks and four

Texas Rangers suddenly busted in and arrested the pugilists (Johnson had to be aided out of the ring, he was still dazed).

The governor had sent Brooks to break up the fight and take the combatants into custody (Roberts, 1983). Even though he really didn't care one way or another about boxing, the governor did care about maintaining the law. Choynski and Johnson were given $5,000 bonds. Unable to pay, the two spent the next three weeks in jail sparing intermittently, as they were encouraged to do by prison authorities, to a captive audience. *"They were forced room-mates for several weeks, and the Sherriff—who loved the manly art—allowed the local boxing club to send Johnson and Choynski boxing gloves which they could use to playfully spar in the yard (Slack, 2015)."*

On March 20th, the judge reduced the bond to $1,000. It was paid two days later and both were freed. Even though the whole ordeal was unusual, it was not as if Johnson hadn't benefited. Sparring with Choynski had taught him a lot: Slipping punches, jabbing, and feigning. In fact, Choynski had been so impressed with Johnson's athleticism he had told him, *"A man who can move like you should never have to take a punch (Ward G. C., 2004)."* The two remained friends for life.

Johnson might have actually taken what Choynski said to heart. He became a beast defensively. Athletic, strong, and fast, he would sometimes block a boxer's thrust with one hand or pull back his body a split second before impact, causing his opponent to be thrown off balance (Barnes P. , Burns, & Schaye, 2004). Johnson's counter-punches would often come from odd angles, which only confounded and confused his prey. This allowed him time to verbally castigate his foes, mentally breaking them down further while at the same time physically breaking them down. Johnson was typically a slow starter in the ring, taking time to measure and study his enemy, before picking up pace later. While quite capable of using his strength for a knockout, he seemed to prefer playing with opponents before battering them into submission. This led some white critics to label him a lazy or an uninspired boxer, although the people who lost to him didn't seem to share that complaint.

Johnson, however, wasn't the only black boxer of his day noted for being supremely superior defensively. This list includes Ed Martin, Sam McVey, Harry Wills, Sam Langford, Peter Jackson, and Joe Jeannette. Roberts (1983) gives an interesting take on why black fighters were generally noted for their defensive styles more so than their white contemporaries: For those black boxers who DID get to fight white boxers, it wasn't a good thing to be too aggressive in the ring. While Whites might tolerate one of their own losing to an African American, they didn't take too kindly to seeing someone White getting utterly destroyed by someone Black. Therefore, a lot of black boxers learned how to *"carry"* white boxers, which required a prodigious use of defensive maneuvers.

Another reason not to be too hard-hitting: It impacted the money flow. *"In part, this was ascribable to economics: a good aggressive black could not get lucrative fights with white boxers. It actually paid a black boxer never to look too strong or too good against a white opponent. Such great fighters as Johnson and Langford often confessed that they carried white boxers and withheld the full measure of their abilities. For them, greatness lay in the ability to just barely defeat a vastly inferior white boxer (Roberts, 1983)."* Since white boxers were not handicapped by such cultural restraints, they were generally more aggressive in the ring.

To illustrate this point, Roberts (1983) analyzes knockout percentages—a strong measure of aggression in boxing—of the top three white heavyweights of the late 1800's, early 1900's, against the top black heavyweights of the same era. *"Three of the heavyweights of the late nineteenth and early twentieth centuries were Sullivan, Sharkey, and Jeffries. Sullivan's knockout percentage was 71 percent, Sharkey's 68, and Jeffries's 71. For the same period the best black heavyweights were Jack Johnson, Sam Langford, Peter Jackson, Joe Jeanette, and Sam McVey. Johnson's knockout percentage was 40 percent, Langford's 39, Jackson's 44, Jeannette's 36, and McVey's 41. Spectators expected white fighters to be aggressive.*

Indeed, James J. Corbett, the white boxer who defeated Sullivan, was roundly criticized for his scientific and defensive style. Black boxers, however, were seldom criticized for their defensive methods (Roberts, 1983)."

Johnson would scour the United States—going to the North and to the South, and then East and West—fighting the top black heavyweight fighters and any white fighter he could, making a name for himself. Soon his efforts began to be recognized nationally. It was during this time, around 1902, that Johnson began *"feeling himself,"* but he had reason to be effusive. Out of 14 fights, he had won 11; three had been a draw. On the West coast, where he had been boxing at the time, he began not paying bills (a habit that would plague him for the rest of his life).

Johnson would also attract the wrong attention for attempting to live in a white section of town. A warrant was issued for both affronts. A statement in the **Bakersfield Daily California** read, *"It is said that Jack has made himself somewhat obnoxious to various persons who…made the charge, claiming that he is living in the forbidden district and beating bills (Roberts, 1983)."* The year would also find Johnson firing his manager, Frank Carrillo, who said he was dismissed because he had gotten in-between Johnson and a woman Johnson was dating. However, Carrillo wouldn't be the only manager fired. Johnson would have a combative relationship with most of his handlers because he didn't trust white men.

"He believed—often on good evidence—that because he was black, whites tried to take advantage of him. Ultimately he viewed managers in the same light as taxi drivers and lawyers: occasionally they were needed, but it was best never to keep one for too long (Robert, 1983)." Speaking of women….

Much has been made of Johnson's love life and his sexual appetites. After watching a bevy of women enter his hotel room, a reporter once asked what was the secret to his prowess. Johnson supposedly replied, *"Eat jellied eels and think distant thoughts (Husband, 2016)."* Of women, Johnson said, *"There have been countless women in my life. They have participated in my triumphs and suffered with me in my moments of disappointment. They have inspired me to attainment and they have balked me; they have caused me joy and they have heaped misery upon me; they have been faithful to the utmost and they have been faithless; they have praised and loved me and they have hated and denounced me. Always, a woman has swayed me — sometimes many have demanded my attention at the same moment (Johnson, 2018)."*

Another aspect of Johnson's life—one often discussed very heatedly—was his predilection for white females, specifically white prostitutes. While it is clear Johnson preferred white women, at least later in his life, he did date black women. In fact, in his book, **My Life In The Ring & Out** (Johnson, 2018), he states he was married five times, the first two being to black females, though as Roberts tells us, Johnson was prone to exaggeration and had a habit of bestowing the title of *"Mrs. Johnson"* on any woman with whom he was living. During one period in Philadelphia, there were supposedly five women claiming to be Mrs. Johnson at the same time!

According to available documentation, however, Johnson was only legally married three times to Etta Terry Duryea in 1911, Lucille Cameron in 1912, and Irene Pineau in 1924. The first two black women Johnson supposedly were married to are Mary Austin, a Galveston native, in 1898, and Clara Kerr (no marriage date given) who was a prostitute from Philadelphia that Johnson met in 1903 (Burns, 2004). Though Johnson states Austin and he were in love, she left him due to a domestic dispute; the relationship with Kerr was more contentious.

Kerr spent time with Johnson in Bakersfield (she had been the woman over which Carrillo was fired) and lived with him for several years. As fate would have it, in 1906 she started an affair with a close friend of Johnson's, a racehorse trainer named William Bryant, and left Johnson for him. Of his friend stabbing him in the back, Johnson retorted, *"I hailed him as an old and intimate friend and invited him to share our home with us. For a time the arrangement was a mutually satisfactory one, but suddenly just when I was congratulating myself on my success, taking the utmost pleasure of Clara in my life, she and Bryant ran away. Unknown to me, an attachment had developed between the two which resulted in their secret preparations to leave together. They took with them all my clothes, all other personal property of mine which was of any value, and disappeared one night when I was giving my attention to my ring affairs (Johnson, 2018)."*

According to his book, Johnson was deeply in love with Kerr: He had to have been to still desire her after betraying him with his friend. Johnson tracked Kerr down and got her back. *"For the first time in my life my faith in friends and humanity had been shaken to the foundation. For a while I debated with myself as to what course I should take. Perhaps I should have let matters go as they were, but the more I thought it over the more I realized how much I esteemed Clara, and I determined that I would not let her get away from me. Having come to this resolve, I set about making inquiries and learned in which direction the couple had fled. Immediately I set out in pursuit. The trail led me to Tucson, Arizona, where I found them. I effected a reconciliation with Clara and we returned to Chicago (Johnson, 2018)."*

Johnson should have let dogs lay. After the reconciliation, Kerr eventually left him again. Yet, this time the reason was more economical. Johnson's money had started running short. One thing to note in the aftermath of the Kerr saga: A possible reason Johnson was swayed towards white women might have been because he had been deeply hurt by a black one. *"After returning from Australia, Johnson began traveling with white women exclusively, writing in his 1927 autobiography that 'the heartaches which Mary Austin and Clara Kerr caused me to forswear colored women and to determine that my lot henceforth would be cast only with white women (Burns, 2004)."*

Of Johnson's supposed marriage to Mary Austin, Roberts (1983) states, *"Certainly a woman named Mary Austin did travel with Johnson for a few years, and he did introduce her as his wife. But they were never legally married. In the 1900 census reports Johnson is listed as a single male living at home with his parents, and no female named Mary lived there (Roberts, 1983)."* In 1909, Johnson met Etta Terry Duryea while on Long Island for the Vanderbilt Cup car race. Duryea, a Brooklyn socialite of *"sporting men,"* was the ex-wife of Charles C. Duryea, who was an Eastern horseracing aficionado. Etta was prone to bouts of depression (Burns, 2004) and being with Johnson wouldn't make things any better. Despite marrying Duryea in 1911, Johnson would still associate with Hattie McClay and Belle Schreiber, both prostitutes from his past. In fact, frequently when Johnson would go out of town in one of his fancy sport cars, all three ladies would join him.

Most often, he would get them separate rooms in the same hotel, or sometimes in a different hotel, and see them individually as he saw fit. *"When Johnson left New York for Philadelphia, Etta went along. So too did Belle and Hattie. The two prostitutes were used to the arrangement, but Etta was not. There were several scenes, but nothing Johnson could not handle. The three stayed in separate hotels and waited for Johnson. That was his normal procedure when traveling with more than one woman. At any time in the day or night he might make a brief appearance for the purpose of intercourse, but he usually left after a short stay. Bell and Hattie, as prostitutes, were accustomed to such behavior. He treated Etta differently. She stayed at the hotel where he stayed. She was, it soon became clear, the number one Mrs. Jack Johnson (Roberts, 1983)."*

Even before Johnson married Duryea, drama was already rampant in the relationship. At one point, he thought she was cheating on him with his French chauffeur, Gaston Le Fort, so he hired a private investigator to follow her. On December 25, 1910, Johnson *"…beat Etta so severely about the face and stomach that she required hospitalization. Nurse Edna Walton, who was on duty the day Etta was admitted to Chicago's Washington Park Hospital, later recalled Etta's blackened and swollen face, the result of an 'accident' suffered while boarding a streetcar (Roberts, 1983)."*

Johnson later sent his close friend Roy Jones to the hospital to make peace with Duryea, so she would not file charges. Evidently, the offer of armistice worked. Johnson and she were wed several weeks later. Yet, to be a white woman and to openly deal with Johnson was to be a woman of no race and of no audience. Duryea claimed that, after she began associating with Johnson, she was shunned by the white world and not openly accepted by the black one, either. Extreme loneliness developed. Though she knew of her husband's infidelities—perhaps even expected it because he was the great *"Jack Johnson"*—she hadn't signed up for the ostracization. She felt trapped.

Adding to Duryea's weariness, her father had died in January 1912. This all led her to a suicidal nadir. On September 11, 1912, she reneged on accompanying a friend to Las Vegas, a trip on which Johnson had encouraged her to go. Duryea's excuse was that she was too sick (Burns, 2004). When he went to change the tickets at the train station, she shot herself in the head with a gun.

"In an almost businesslike fashion she made a few telephone calls, said goodbye to several friends, and then, after asking that they pray for her, dismissed her two maids. Alone in her bedroom, she held one of Johnson's guns to her right temple and squeezed the trigger (Roberts, 1983)." Not letting any grass grow under his feet, Johnson married Lucille Cameron just three months later, on December 4, 1912. During the summer, Cameron had come to work for Johnson as a stenographer at his club in Chicago, the **Café de Champion** (discussed briefly in the next chapter). Although 18 years old when Johnson hired her, Cameron had already been an experienced prostitute in Minneapolis.

"Johnson later wrote that their relationship was 'purely of a business nature and devoid of undue intimacy.' Perhaps it was a business relationship, but Lucille's business was intimacy (Roberts, 1983)." Cameron proved to be more resilient than Duryea. She also proved to be extremely loyal. In the early stages, when the United States Government was attempting to convict Johnson of the Mann Act, she refused to testify. Of course, this was the least she could do. Her mother had initially been the cause of Johnson's legal problems. Cameron and he would eventually divorce in 1924 because of Johnson's infidelities.

Later that fall, he would meet two women at a racetrack in Aurora, Illinois: Irene Pineau and Helen Matthews. Sometime at the beginning of the year, Pineau divorced her husband and both Matthews and she began dating Johnson together. Pineau won out and Johnson and she married in August 1925. She was with Johnson until his death in 1946. At her husband's funeral, she was asked what she loved about him. Pineau's reply, *"I loved him because of his courage. He faced the world unafraid. There wasn't anybody or anything he feared (Burns, 2004)."*

Because of his open association with white women—because of his open association with *"questionable"* white women—Johnson was disreputable in the white community. *"Though many hated Jack Johnson simply because he was a black conqueror of 'white hopes,' much of the prejudice against him can be explained in his relations with white women (Gilmore, 1973)."* Other heavyweight boxers, such as Sam McVeigh and Sam Langford, associated with white women, too, but they had the discretion not to court them in public (Roberts, 1983). Not Johnson. Whatever he did, he always did in grand style.

Particularly after he won the Heavyweight title in 1908, to say he was hated by white America, would be an understatement. He was not simply disliked. He. Was. Abhorred! It was almost as if Mede (Johnson) had proved he was physically superior to the white man and had gone on to ravage all of Master Hammond's wives (if he had had more than one). *"After Johnson married Cameron, two ministers in the South recommended that Johnson be lynched and racists looked for a way to punish Jack Johnson (Jack Johnson, n.d.)."*

It was one thing for white men to be bested in the ring by this Brute, but to have their women pillaged by him, too? The affront was too much to bear. White America worked feverously to find a conspiracy. Nothing it had done to curtail his arrogance so far had worked. Infatuated with fast and fancy cars, Johnson was frequently cited for running red lights and stop signs. He always feigned ignorance and was able to buy himself out of trouble. If he beat someone up due to a dispute, he either paid the party off under the table or he reluctantly paid the fine (Roberts, 1983). Seemingly no monkey-wrench the power structure hurled at him curtailed his momentum. Even the press couldn't shame Johnson into submission. As a black man, he was used to the hatred. As a black man who was perhaps the most feared in America, he somewhat expected it, maybe even wanted it. Fortunately for him, there was always vitriol to be found.

The *"big black"* and *"the big negro"*: These are words the **New York Times** utilized in describing Johnson in his day (Eligon & Thorpe, *Missed in Coverage of Jack Johnson, the Racism Around Him*, 2018). To a certain extent, such rhetoric was expected from the mainstream press. Yet, even a lot of African Americans were appalled by his behavior and called him worse. They felt his flashy clothes, lifestyle, outspokenness, and open seduction of white females would bring on unduly hardships to Blacks as Whites sought retribution, and in some respects they were right.

CHASED BY CROWDS

ATLANTA, Ga., July 4.—Rioting started here soon after the result of the fight became known. Many negroes were chased by the crowds.

THREE INJURED

HOUSTON, Texas, July 4.—Rioting broke out tonight on the announcement of Johnson's victory at Reno. Three negroes were badly hurt by white men inside of an hour. Police were called to quell several minor disturbances.

NEGROES ATTACK WOMAN

FORT WORTH, Texas, July 4.—Minor disturbances between whites and blacks broke out here following the announcement of Johnson's victory this afternoon. The most serious attack was made by two negroes with beer bottles on a white woman.

SHOOTINGS AT LITTLE ROCK

LITTLE ROCK, July 4.—Lee Roberts, an Iron Mountain passenger conductor, was shot and wounded during a fight on his train between three white men and negroes today immediately following the result of the Reno fight. Two negroes are reported killed by white men, one by a Rock Island conductor coming into this city tonight and the other in town.

Newspaper headlines from July 4, 1910, after Jack Johnson
successfully defended his title against Jim Jeffries

One of Johnson's greatest pundits during this time became Booker T. Washington, a black intellectual conservative and the ultimate accommodationist for white America (Johnson must have been really doing something wrong—or maybe right—if Washington was condemning him). *"Booker T. Washington believed that Jack Johnson was an embarrassment to his race and only succeeded in hindering efforts to further improve the economic and social status of African-Americans within American society."* Washington would say the following in the **Baltimore Afro-American Ledger** in 1912:

> *It is unfortunate that a man with money should use it in a way to injures his own people in the eyes of those who are seeking to uplift his race and improve its conditions…. In misrepresenting the colored people of this country, this man is harming himself the least. Jack Johnson has harmed rather than helped the race. I wish to say emphatically that his actions do not meet with the approval of the colored race. Johnson, fortunate or rather unfortunate, it seems in the possession of money, is doing a grave injustice to his race…. Undoubtedly Johnson's actions are repudiated by the great majority of right-thinking people of the Negro race (Washington, 1912)."*

Many conservative Blacks implored Washington to see if he could reason with Johnson, get him to tone things down. Johnson rejected Washington's pleas, as if his words were otiose. However, just two years earlier, the **New York Age**, a paper sympathetic to Washington, asked Johnson to:

> *"Conduct himself in a modest manner. He can hurt the race immeasurably just now if he goes splurging and making a useless noisy exhibition of himself. We hope that he will not be arrested on any charge. Any undue exhibition on the part of Mr. Johnson will hurt every member of the race; on the other hand, becoming modesty and self-control will win him many lasting friends (Advice To Jack Johnson, 1910)."*

If only he had followed the **New York Age's** advice, perhaps the next few years wouldn't have been so tumultuous for Johnson, but then again, if he had followed the paper's advice…he would have never become the first black Heavyweight Champion.

Chapter Three
The Great White Hope

"The reason Jack Johnson was so beset by his own country, a country ironically which had only recently reaffirmed that all men were created equal, was because of his Unforgivable Blackness."

W.E.B. DuBois

People could say what they wanted to about Johnson—that maybe he partied and drank too much, that maybe he loved *"women of the night"* too much—but what they couldn't say was that he didn't know how to handle himself in the ring. On February 3, 1903, he won the Negro Heavyweight title (Blacks had to have their own Heavyweight title, since they couldn't fight Whites for theirs) when he beat Denver Ed Martin on points in 20 rounds, despite being outweighed by 23lbs (Roberts, 1983). Even before this, Johnson had already begun audaciously eyeing the Heavyweight title, despite no black man ever having been allowed to fight for it.

At the time, the Heavyweight Champion was James J. Jeffries, also known as the *"Boilermaker."* Jeffries, who won the Heavyweight title from Bob Fitzsimmons on June 9, 1899, is *"...still regarded by some fight historians as the single greatest heavyweight in history, was a fearsome and intimidating fighter who established plenty of credentials for himself in just 21 professional prizefights. He was the very embodiment of the rugged, two-fisted hulk of brawn that people at the turn of the century wanted their champion to be (James J. Jefferies, n.d.)."*

Initially, it seemed Johnson and Jeffries would never meet, at least in the ring. The white champion refused to consider a match against the black boxer, even as African Americans called on him to do so. Johnson attempted to instigate the matter, publicly challenging him, but Jeffries wouldn't take the bait. In 1904, he stated *"I don't care whether Johnson licks the Japanese army... I have repeatedly declared that, so long as I am in the fighting business, I will never make a match with a black man. The negroes may come and the negroes may go, and some of the negroes may be excellent fighting men. Just tell the public that James J. Jeffries has made up his mind that he will never put on boxing gloves to battle an Ethiopian (Ward G. C., 2004)."*

Then, on May 2, 1905, Jeffries seemingly did the impossible. He retired, which was rare for a boxing champion. No other Heavyweight had ever done so. All had been defeated in the ring, with the crown passed down to the winner. Consequently, unlike most involved in the sport, Jeffries was a bit different. He had initially gotten into fighting because of the money, not necessarily for an innate love of boxing and it was a convenient time to get out of the game.

Politically, prizefighting had come under attack, with the earnings becoming a little too skimpy. Jeffries didn't see the point of getting hit upside the head—even if he was the champion—if the money wasn't going to be right. He quit boxing and tried to fall into a quiet life of farming. *"Progressive attacks on boxing had begun by 1905 to deplete the interest in the sport. And as interest, especially of the wealthy, declined, so too did the size of purses. The profession was going broke (Roberts, 1983)."*

Since there was no boxing commission around to handle the transition of the title to a ranked contender, it was soon decided the retiring champion would pick the next two fighters who would meet for the title: Jack Root and Marvin Hart. In a lack luster pugilistic encounter on July 3, 1905, in Reno, Nevada, Hart knocked out Root in the 12th round. Yet, Hart would soon prove he was no Jeffries (or not even a mirror of Jeffries' shadow); he would lose the championship in 1906 in his first title defense to Canadian Heavyweight Tommy Burns. This in turn set the stage for Johnson to direct all of his energies pressuring Burns to a fight.

Despite the expression, *"trolling someone,"* not yet being in existence, this is in essence what Johnson did. For a period of two years, sitting ringside, he chased Burns around the world, buying tickets to his boxing matches, insolently inviting him to fight. Burns continued to rebuke Johnson, but it soon became more an issue about money and less about crossing the color line. Johnson was selling too many wolf tickets for Burns to ignore.

"How does Burns want it? Does he want it fast and willing? I'm his man in that case. Does he want it flat footed? Goodness, if he does, why I'm his man again. Anything to suit; but fast or slow, I'm going to win (Broome, 1979)." Eventually, Burns was given an offer he couldn't refuse. Color line be damned: He jumped over it! White detractors immediately began to denounce Burns, labelling him a turncoat and traitor. It didn't matter. Money talked and everything else walked. "The champion happily pocketed the huge sum and ignored the outcry from those who insisted he was betraying the white race and tarnishing the world title. Seemingly confident of his superiority over Johnson, Burns declared: 'I will beat Johnson, or my name isn't Tommy Burns.' Whether he was being ironic at the time will never be known; 'Tommy Burns' had in fact been born 'Noah Brusso' (Garcia, 2019)."

To get around segregation laws, the fight was held in Sydney, Australia (Husband, 2016). For the bout, Burns received $30,000, the largest cash prize for boxing up to that point (Christie, n.d.), and Johnson $5,000. The obvious lopsided nature of the purse (the equivalent of $844,894.00 and $140,815.00 in today's money, respectively) mattered naught to Johnson. His mind was set on the long game. He also was not going to be denied what was his to take. The two boxers met on December 26, 1908, at the Sydney Stadium at Rushcutters Bay.

In front of a hostile, mostly white audience of 20,000 (30,000 were thought to be outside the stadium, unable to get in), Johnson gave Burns the beating of his life. Of course, his trademark grin was on full display. "At one point, Johnson invited Burns, who had defended his title against 12 men leading up to this bout, to hit as hard as he possibly could. Johnson opened his arms as if to hug the man, who stood 7 inches shorter and 24 pounds lighter, and allowed him to hit him. Johnson barely flinched, and his point to Burns and the crowd was made loud and clear: He didn't fear Burns, and this fight was going to end once he finally decided to actually fight (Walker, 2017)."

Perhaps it was a good thing, then, that law enforcement was on hand to reign in the unruly crowd. Jeffries had offered to referee the contest for $5,000, but the promoter, Hugh

"Huge Deal" McIntosh, thought this a tad too much (Christie, n.d.). Instead, McIntosh refereed the fight himself (Tommy Burns vs. Jack Johnson, 2017). Johnson received a few cheers from the audience, but was more readily greeted with words such as *"coon"* and *"nigger,"* which were hurled with effortless impunity.

In terms of physicality, the match was over before it even began. *"When the two battlers entered the ring, the physical superiority of Johnson was immediately apparent. Having trained rigorously at Rushcutters Bay, the challenger was in splendid condition (Garcia, 2019)."* From the very beginning, Johnson set the tone, taunting Burns, *"Poor little Tommy, who told you you were a fighter (Tommy Burns vs. Jack Johnson, 2017)?"* Burns was floored in the first round. In the second and fourth, Johnson arrogantly turned his back toward him and began talking to the crowd (Garcia, 2019).

Whenever Burns did land a punch, Johnson would say things like, *"Poor, poor, Tommy. Who taught you to hit? Your mother (Tommy Burns vs. Jack Johnson, 2017)?"* The match continued, completely one-sided, as if a 13-year old boy with developing acne was attempting to fight a grown man. Johnson effortlessly whupped Burns, so much that he was able to continuously turn his attention to the crowd to engage them, but all he did was make them angrier. *"When Johnson was not insulting Burns, he was talking to ringsiders. Usually he just joked about how easy the fight was and what he would do with the money he won from betting on the bout. That the ringsiders hated Johnson and screamed racial insults did not seem to bother him (Roberts, 1983)."*

By the 14th round, Burns was so battered, bloodied, and bruised, the police stepped in to stop the fight. The white crowd could take no more. Yet, the unthinkable had occurred: The Heavyweight title was now in the clutches of a black man. Mede had taken over the plantation! Writing for the **New York Herald**, novelist Jack London, who was a bit of a negrophobe and on hand to view the spectacle, wrote, *"The fight!—There was no fight! . . . It had all the seeming of a playful Ethiopian at loggerheads with a small white man—of a grown man* *cuffing with a naughty child—of a monologue by Johnson who made a noise with his fist like a lullaby, tucking Burns into a crib (London, 1908)."*

He then called on the former champ to come out of retirement to deal with the black interloper. *"But one thing now remains. Jim Jeffries must emerge from his alfalfa farm and remove the golden smile from Jack Johnson's face. Jeff, it's up to you! The White Man must be rescued (Walker, 2017)."* By closing out his statement with, *"The White Man must be rescued,"* London, like much of white American, viewed Johnson's victory as one in a battle against the white race. The Brute had just proved that he was physically better and this was something that would not be tolerated.

"London and the multitudes who echoed his call thus cast Jeffries as a 'white hope' who would put Johnson—and by extension the African-American population he represented—back in his subordinate place (Vogan, 2010)." For his part, Jeffries was highly critical and very vocal of Burns losing the title. He espoused the belief the fight never should have taken place, and inserted false bravado. In a column for the **Scone Advocate**, he wrote, *"Burns has sold his pride, the pride of the Caucasian race. … The Canadian never will be forgiven by the public for allowing the title of the best physical man in the world to be wrested from his keeping by a member of the African race. I refused time and again to meet Johnson while I was holding the title, even though I knew I could beat him. I would never allow a Negro a chance to fight for the world's championship, and I advise all other champions to follow the same course. … All night long I was besieged with telegrams asking me to re-enter the ring. I answer them now as I have answered them hundreds of times: 'I have fought my last fight' (Walker, 2017)."*

Thus, began the call for a Great White Hope to defeat Johnson and regain the Heavyweight title. Johnson stayed in Australia for a while after the fight, joining a vaudeville show, which was not unusual for boxers in that day and age. Because of Aussie curiosity, he actually made more money touring with the show than from his $5,000 payday with Burns. Already proud and stubborn before winning the title, now more than ever Johnson was determined to be his own man on his own terms. *"Starting in 1909 the American public began to see the Bad Nigger in Johnson. They saw the way in which he challenged white authority in his numerous brushes with the law. They heard the stories of his night life, the lurid talks of his week-long drunks and parties. Tales of his sexual bouts were also told, and his shaved head came to symbolize the sexual virility of the black male. But most shocking of all were the times he appeared in public with white women (Roberts, 1983)."*

It was enough of a travesty Johnson was now Heavyweight Champion, but for him to flaunt white women so openly? The REALLY messed up part was that Johnson did everything in style. This was like rubbing salt in the womb. Consummate showman that he was, his suits were tailor made of the finest materials; his vehicles, the most expensive a person could buy. Even the club in Chicago Johnson later owned in 1912—the Café De Champion at 41 W. 31st St. in Bronzeville—was of one of the most exquisite. Supposedly, the establishment cost $30,000 to open and served things as exotic and unique as caviar sandwiches, two for $.60 (Wine Flows Like Lapaloma Melody, 1912).

"The monogrammed spittoons were said to be solid silver. Fifteen thousand dollars' worth of oil paintings of the owner and his family hung on the walls, and mosaic inlaid tile covered the floor from front to back. Its 'auspicious inaugural function' — a 'grand opening' was deemed too plebeian for such a palace — overshadowed the Republican National Convention, one newspaper wrote (Johnson C. J., 2018)."

The club, a *"black and tan"* (meaning, a desegregated place where Blacks and Whites mingled together), became a source of pride within the black community. *"By all accounts, the club ran smoothly from the start. Johnson's wife, Etta Terry Duryea Johnson — a white woman — helped run the restaurant operations. White-gloved waiters in evening clothes shuffled food to the tables in the main room, near the lavish mahogany bar and to the private dining area on the second floor. The Pompeiian Room, which hosted musicians and dancers, could hold hundreds, it was reported (Johnson C. J., 2018)."*

Upstairs, there were offices and private rooms where Johnson *"entertained"* some of his special guests. The upstairs of the Café De Champion also contained an apartment, which is where Duryea had committed suicide. Although the short-lived club became a source of inspiration for the black community, it was probably another affront to white racist sensibilities and another warning that Johnson was *"dangerous."* The symbolism of Café De' Champion cannot be denied. It was impunity unleashed, an extravagance that could inspire the black masses to *"forget their place"* in the natural order of America's social hierarchy and rise up.

"Privately and publicly many blacks applauded Johnson's exploits because he defied all of the degrading customs of America. He was rich when most blacks were poor; free to do as he chose when most blacks were circumscribed' and braggadocious [sic] when many blacks were forced to bear their oppression in silence (Blassingame, 1975)."

Unfortunately, besting Johnson was easier said than done. Every Great White Hope brought before had been dispatched with relative ease. Through each win, Johnson's legend and arrogance grew. Eventually, all roads led back to Jeffries who, by 1909, when he began to consider fighting Johnson, was five years into his retirement. Perhaps it was the allure of the money—the amount stood to be made was staggering—or maybe he was tired of reading the myriad letters begging him to unretire and put the black buck in his place. Regardless, he had decided to become the new Great White Hope.

"Hundreds of letters were sent to Jeffries with a single theme: it was incumbent upon him as a white man to shut Johnson's smiling mouth once and for all. White Americans doubted not that Jeffries was up to the task. They believed the Jeffries mythology—that he cured himself of pneumonia by drinking a case of whisky in two days, that with a broken leg he was still able to knock out a leading heavyweight contender, that upon inspection a physician told him that he was simply not human (Roberts, 1983)."

There was an immediate problem, though, a really BIG problem (besides Jeffries being a hypocrite for doing the same thing he accused Burns of doing). Having not boxed in several years, Jeffries had ballooned to 300lbs! When he had been actively fighting, the 6'2 Jeffries weighed 210lbs. Preparing to bring Johnson to heel, he would come in at 227lbs, proclaiming, *"That portion of the white race that has been looking at me to defend its athletic supremacy may feel assured that I am fit to do my very best (McCormick, 2020)."*

However, another problem presented itself along the way. Despite much of America clamoring to see the fight, there were many who did not. Perhaps they were fearful of another Burns debacle? Johnson's ego didn't need to get any larger. Although the person who promoted the fight, George *"Tex"* Rickard, originally planned to host the contest in San Francisco, the Governor of California was persuaded politically not to allow it there (Racism Takes a Blow in Reno, n.d.). Post haste, the fight was switched to Reno, Nevada.

"No advertising genius was needed to market the Johnson-Jeffries fight. The issues in this fight were literally black and white. Rickard felt no qualms about exploiting the race issue. Jeffries became the 'Hope of the White Race' and Johnson the 'Negroes' Deliverer' (Roberts, 1983)." The winner was guaranteed two-thirds of $101,000 (McCormick, 2020), with movie revenue also to be split, although Johnson's film share would be significantly less if he won. The movie would be worth less. White Americans wouldn't pay to see a film showing a black man beating up a white man.

Jeffries was favored in the fight seven - 10, but despite shedding his dad bod to get back in shape, aesthetically, Johnson was grander. *"Regardless of Johnson's superior conditioning and recent successes, few dared to bet on him. Jim Corbett believed Jeffries would win, as did George Little, Johnson's former manager. At the Reno betting parlour operated by Corbett's brother Tom, there was no one willing to wager on a Jack Johnson victory. Betting with their hearts, few, if any, members of the white public were willing to place their financial faith in a black man's claim to athletic supremacy (McCormick, 2020)."*

Johnson was often his most dangerous when he was smiling. Those betting against him should have been paying better attention to the days leading up to the fight. Johnson was smiling effusively, from ear to ear, like a Cheshire cat. He was relaxed at his training camp at Seal Beach, talking and joking with newspaper writers.

Prior to the fight, the media attempted to make Jeffries out to be the savoir and Johnson a savage, as if the latter were an animal. *"Within the fight's white supremacist environment there was a clear racial division of the boxers in terms of heroism and villainy. Jeffries was portrayed by the white establishment as courageous, disciplined, civilized and solid, while Johnson was 'yellow,' savage, a braggart and a drinker. Detractors represented Johnson as primitive and gorilla-like, in asserting his supposedly innate inferiority, while also taking issue with his nonchalant and carefree demeanor during training camp (Alderman, Inwood, & Tyner, 2018)."*

Ironically, the fight—scheduled for 45 rounds—would be held on July 4, 1910, though it would not be an Independence Day in the boxing ring for white America. Some of the same hostile elements, from when Johnson had fought Burns two years earlier in Sydney, were in play in Reno. To minimize violence, the sale of alcohol on the site was prohibited and firearms were collected before entry (Racism Takes a Blow in Reno, n.d.).

Twenty-five thousand people were on hand as the rest of America held its collective breath. Even at Tuskegee Institute in Tuskegee, Alabama, Booker T. Washington allowed students access to a wire telegraph so they could monitor the fight (Riemann, 2017). Outside the New York Times building, approximately 30,000 people—most of them White—did the same: Waited around for telegraph updates to be apprised of the status of the fight (Fetter, 2010). As Johnson made his way to the ring, the band launched into a song called **"All Coons Look Alike to Me."** The crowd would also begin reciting, *"Kill the nigger (Parthun, 2009)."*

The 32-year-old Johnson started off slowly against the 35-year-old Jeffries. Despite Jeffries landing a few punches, he couldn't adequately penetrate Johnson's defenses. Even when the two clinched, though Jeffries had the advantage in mass, Johnson had the advantage in strength. The **New York Times** would write, *"After the third round Johnson treated his* *opponent almost as a joke. He smiled and blocked playfully, warding off rushes of Jeffries with a marvellous science, now tucking a blow under his arm, again plucking it out of the air as a man stops a baseball (Sad Crowd at Ringside, 1910)."* This might have merely been the measuring of Jeffries' might and offensive skills. Or had Johnson been thinking about his film revenue? Regardless, he later began picking up the pace.

"Most of the reporters believed that Johnson could have ended the fight in an early round. They said he did not because he was a good businessman and a vengeful person. Financially a quick fight would have been disastrous. It would have destroyed the potential of the film as a revenue source. But beyond the money question, reporters believed Johnson enjoyed watching Jeffries suffer. By round twelve Jeffries' mouth was cut inside and out; his nose was broken and bleeding; his face and eyes were bruised and smeared with blood. Even Johnson's chest and back were covered with Jeffries' blood. There was no reason for the fight to go on. But it did (Roberts, 1983)."

In the 14th round, the once indestructible Jeffries was floored by Johnson three times. Punch drunk, though willing to continue, Jeffries' team conceded the fight by throwing in the towel by the 15th. They had to save their fighter's dignity. *"Amid cries of 'Don't let the nigger knock him out!' Jeffries' corner stopped the fight to prevent further damage, both physical and figurative. White fans rushed the ring after the stoppage, but Johnson's men formed a protective barrier around the champion. No one questioned the outcome or the fact that Johnson had proven himself the better man. Tellingly, Jeffries himself admitted he could never have beaten Johnson, even in his prime. 'I could never have whipped Johnson at my best,' he said. 'I couldn't have hit him. No, I couldn't have reached him in a thousand years' (McCormick, 2020)."*

Johnson's total from revenues associated with the fight were $117,000.00 (some sources say $145,000.00) the equivalent of $3,191,033.00 today. The aftermath would find everyone—Black and White—losing their collective minds. While there was no bloodshed on the scale of the Red Summer of 1919, *"...post-fight riots erupted in cities and towns throughout the nation including Washington, Philadelphia, Little Rock,*

St. Joseph (Missouri), New Orleans, Baltimore, Cincinnati, Louisville, Roanoke, St. Louis, Macon (Georgia), Pueblo (Colorado), as well as New York City itself (Fetter, 2010)." Apparently, it was bad news to be Black and in a celebratory mood. In retaliation for Johnson winning the fight, white mobs killed over 150 African Americans (Parthun, 2009). Stories from that day sound like something out of a dark comedy.

"Charles Williams, a negro fight enthusiast, had his throat slashed from ear to ear on a streetcar by a white man, having announced too vociferously his appreciation of Jack Johnson's victory in Reno (Negro Enthusiast Killed, 1910)." Black educator Benjamin Mays, who was 14 at the time of Johnson's victory over Jeffries, stated, *"White men in my country could not take it [when Johnson defeated Jeffries]…Negroes dared not discuss the outcome of this match in the presence of whites. In fact, Johnson's victory was hard on the white man's world….Jack Johnson committed two grave blunders as far as whites were concerned: He beat up a white man and he was socializing with a white woman—both deadly (Gilmore A. , 1975)."* White mobs in Atlanta harassed Blacks, while several white men in New York set fire to a tenement building where Blacks lived and blocked the main exits (Domonoske, 2018) (Riemann, 2017).

"In Washington, two white men were fatally stabbed by black men, with 236 people arrested in that city alone. And in Omaha, a black man was smothered to death in a barber's chair, while in Wheeling, West Virginia, a black man driving an expensive car — just as the playboyish Jack Johnson was famous for — was beset by a mob and hanged (Riemann, 2017)." Of the rampant violence, the *Chicago Defender* took the position that it was better *"…for Johnson to win and a few Negroes to have been killed in body for it, than for Johnson to have lost and all Negroes to have been killed in spirit by the preachments of inferiority from the combined white press. The fact of this fight will outdo a mountain peak of theory about the Negro as a physical man, - and as a man of self-control and courage (Pickens, 1910)."*

While prizefighting films were already controversial in many circles—due to the Progressives' attack on morality— images of the Jeffries' loss were particularly abhorred. Congress had already attempted to ban the distribution of prizefighting films in 1897, after footage of the Corbett-Fitzsimmons fight emerged. Despite the bill failing, interest was renewed in the prohibition once Johnson's dark-skinned, smiling face materialized on the screen.

"Whereas prizefighting films in general were perceived to be a threat to the public good during this time, images of Johnson dominating white opponents were deemed wholly unfit for circulation and public exhibition. After Johnson's 1908 heavyweight title-winning fight against Tommy Burns, theaters throughout the country and world refused to show or were pressured to suppress films of the match. Fight film suppression became even more widespread and vigilantly enforced after Johnson's successful 1910 title defense against 'white hope' Jim Jeffries—a fight whose outcome provoked racially-motivated violence throughout the United States (Vogan, 2010)."

In fact, many cities down South outright refused to show the Jeffries-Johnson contest and legislation was passed to hamper its distribution. President Theodore Roosevelt chimed, *"The last contest provoked a very unfortunate display of race antagonism. I sincerely trust that public sentiment will be so aroused, and will make itself felt so effectively, as to guarantee that this is the last prize fight to take place in the United States and it would be an admirable thing if some method could be devised to stop the exhibition of the moving pictures taken thereof (Roosevelt Condemns Fight, 1910)."* Studying this moment in time, W.E.B. DuBois would later reflect in 1914, somewhat sarcastically, *"Boxing has fallen into disfavor...The cause is clear: Jack Johnson...Neither he nor his race invented prize fighting or particularly like it. Why then this thrill of national disgust? Because Johnson is black...Wherefore we conclude that at present prize fighting is very, very immoral ... until Mr. Johnson retires or permits himself to be 'knocked out' (DuBois, 1914)."*

Unable to stop Johnson in the ring, the power structure sought to use another method of usurpation: The law. Their vehicle of entrapment? One of the things most coveted by Johnson. White women. After Duryea's demise, when Lucille Cameron publicly began appearing on Johnson's arm, her mother contacted the police in Chicago. Embarrassed Cameron was openly cavorting with a Negro in public, she wanted the authorities to do something about it. Couldn't they simply arrest him? The situation was making her family look bad (as if her daughter being a prostitute wasn't problematic enough).

"On Oct. 17, 1912, a woman identified only as 'Mrs. F. Cameron-Falconet' went to the Clark Street police station and, as the Tribune reported, asked the Chicago cops to rescue her daughter, 19 and white, 'from the clutches of Jack Johnson, Negro heavyweight champion pugilist' (Grossman, 2018)." While the police told Cameron-Falconet there was nothing they could do because the relationship was consensual, they began looking for another way to legally ensnare Johnson. They quickly found one: The Mann Act of 1910. They would try to frame him on abduction charges. The day after Cameron-Falconet went to the police station, Johnson was arrested.

"He had been in jail before, and he was not particularly frightened by the police. When he was arrested at noon he laughed, telling reporters that he had too much money to remain long in jail. And indifferent. The charge was not speeding or even smuggling. Those violations could be circumvented with enough cash. This time it was a serious federal violation. From the first the Bureau of Investigation, the predecessor of the Federal Bureau of Investigation, had decided to press for a Mann Act conviction (Roberts, 1983)." While it may be hard for many to accept, they must understand that, prior to the 20th century, prostitution was allowed and even accepted in many municipalities throughout the United States (McNeill, 2017). Yet, because of the Progressives' attack on morality at the close of the era, cities began banning the sex trade.

"By the end of the first decade of the 20th century, America was consumed with a moral fervor to 'rescue' helpless damsels in distress from sex and autonomy. 'White slavery' became a popular theme of books, plays and the new motion pictures, and politicians were close behind; in 1910 Congress passed the infamously-vague White Slave Traffic Act (better known as the Mann Act), and in the next four years literally every American state criminalized prostitution itself, regardless of whether the woman was coerced. Before 1910, the actual transaction was not illegal in any state; by the end of 1914, it was illegal in all of them.

To be sure, brothels were officially tolerated beyond that date in several places (New Orleans until 1917, Honolulu until 1944), and unofficially in many others for decades (New York Mayor La Guardia's campaign against adult businesses in the mid-1930s demonstrated how common they were there). But in general, prostitution in the United States was marginalized and persecuted from that point onward (McNeill, 2017)."

The history of legalized prostitution in America should not come as a surprise to anyone; during the Civil War, the Union army experimented with prostitutes as a way to keep down venereal disease amongst troops (Blakemore, 2019). While many today may look at Johnson's relationships with *"working women"* as immoral, they must understand that *"working women"* were acceptable, at least legally during his era. Though the Mann Act has been somewhat clarified over the years, when it was first introduced, its wording was ambiguous and far-reaching.

Progressives reasoned that part of the problem with prostitution was the sheer number of young immigrant women who were coming to America and being forced into the industry. To combat this, the Mann Act reasoned that preventing immoral acts from crossing state lines would keep *"...innocent girls from being lured into prostitution, but really offered a way to make a crime out of many kinds of consensual sexual activity (Congress passes Mann Act aimed at curbing sex trafficking, 2020)."* Many Whites viewed the concept of miscegenation—the sexual mixing of races—as disturbing, if not downright reprehensible. The Mann Act became one way of keeping black men away from white women.

"In 1917, the Supreme Court upheld the conviction of two married California men, Drew Caminetti and Maury Diggs, who had gone on a romantic weekend getaway with their girlfriends to Reno, Nevada, and had been arrested. Following this decision, the Mann Act was used in all types of cases: someone was charged with violating the Mann Act for bringing a woman from one state to another in order to work as a chorus girl in a theater; wives began using the Mann Act against girls

who ran off with their husbands. The law was also used for racist purposes: Jack Johnson, heavyweight champion of the world, was prosecuted for bringing a prostitute from Pittsburgh to Chicago, but the motivation for his arrest was public outrage over his marriages to white women (Congress passes Mann Act aimed at curbing sex trafficking, 2020)."

The only saving grace of the legislation was that it was not to be used in matters where profit was not a motive. In theory, if no money was exchanged or profit was made—though the *"immoral act"* might have occurred across state lines—a person couldn't be prosecuted. Of the 2,801 people convicted under the Mann Act from 1910 – 1920, 98% of the cases involved money for sex. However, as Roberts says, *"For Jack Johnson, the government was willing to make an exception. In Chicago, United States District Attorney James J. Wilkerson told reporters that Johnson had clearly violated the letter of the Mann Act (Roberts, 1983)."*

As early as 1910, after passage of the Mann Act, authorities were already looking for ways it could be used against Johnson (Burns, *Unforgiveable Blackness: Jack Johnson and the Law,* 2004). As regards the government's abduction allegation, the prosecution attempted to portray Cameron as an innocent girl who was lured to Chicago into a sordid lifestyle by Johnson and his lackeys. Through trumped up charges, it wanted to prove Johnson was some sort of interstate pimp who was in the business of sex trafficking. However, during the trial, it came out that Cameron was a prostitute BEFORE she had even met Johnson and that no one had *"coerced"* her into anything.

"Lucille denied this elaborate conspiracy theory as patently absurd. She admitted that she was a prostitute, which slightly contradicted an earlier claim that she was a virgin, but refused to implicate Johnson in her profession in any way. When the questioning became more specific, Lucille began to sob and fell into a 'hysterical' fit. At that point the grand jury adjourned for the day, and Lucille was released into the custody of her mother (Roberts, 1983)."

Round one went to Johnson. The government's case, weak from the start, was crumbling. However, it would soon find a star witness, one with an axe to grind: Belle Schreiber. To some degree, Schreiber was still in her feelings at Duryea having been crowned Mrs. Jack Johnson over her. On November 7, 1912, she talked to a grand jury, telling them about her times with Johnson. Supposedly, she was very loquacious and convincing. *"After hearing Belle's testimony, the grand jury called for an indictment. Its decision was passed on to Judge Kennesaw Mountain Landis, the no-nonsense dispenser of justice, who promptly issued a bench warrant for Johnson's arrest. Specifically, the champion was charged with transporting Belle from Pittsburgh to Chicago on August 10, 1910, for the purpose of prostitution and debauchery (Roberts, 1983)."*

Johnson bonded out and a trial date was set for May 1913. Because the grand jury had indicted him on a different set of allegations, the abduction charges were dropped on November 20, 1912 (Gilmore A.-T. , *Jack Johnson and White Women: The National Impact*, 1973). On December 4, 1912, he and Cameron were married. Eventually, Johnson was indicted on 11 counts under the Mann Act—from debauchery and unlawful sexual intercourse, to crimes against nature—which mostly pertained to trips Schreiber and he made between Chicago and Milwaukee in late 1910 (Roberts, 1983).

During the early part of the ordeal, Johnson sometimes became defensive, particularly when it came to him justifying his preference for white women. *"I am not a slave and . . . I have the right to choose who my mate shall be without the dictation of any man. I have eyes and I have a heart, and when they fail to tell me who I shall have for mine I want to be put away in a lunatic asylum. So long as I do not interfere with any other man's wife I shall claim the right to select the woman of my own choice. Nobody else can do that for me (Champion Jack Johnson Denies Charges Against him in the Daily Newspapers, 1912)."*

White America lashed out at Johnson. The trial raised their ire to a new level. The following quote helps one to understand the height of their pissitivity. *"During the trial in Chicago, protesters hanged Johnson in effigy. A dummy with its face blackened with paint swung from a tree and included a placard reading 'This is what we will do for Jack Johnson.' Three weeks later, a group in Midland, Texas, sent a letter to the prosecuting attorney, informing him that if he killed Johnson, they'd contribute $100,000 for his defense. When rumors spread of Johnson's assassination — either by a white woman or her relatives, depending on the version — several newspapers published regrets that the boxer remained alive. When a reporter informed Johnson of the rumor, he replied, 'Do I look dead?' (Franco R. J., 2017)."*

Gilmore (1973) writes that while many Blacks were in Johnson's corner prior to his federal trial, there were those who turned against him because of it. Already dismayed by his open preference for white women, African Americans could not understand why Johnson would marry another white female so soon after his first wife had committed suicide. Did he like playing with fire? He was in trouble, in part, because of his affiliations with white women. Some Blacks viewed Johnson as a man attempting to dig his own

A black and white photographic postcard of the "Fight of the Century" between Jack Johnson and James Jeffries.

grave while killing himself at the same time. According to the African American press, he was making the race look bad.

"At the outset of the Johnson-Cameron controversy, many blacks were as antagonistic toward the champion as were whites. More than anything else, it was Johnson's continued open preference for white women that aroused their anger. Strangely enough, much of the anti-Johnson rhetoric was similar to that of whites... 'What a pity,' wrote the **Newport News (Virginia) Star***, 'that Johnson was ever successful in obtaining the great amount of money which came to him, if it is to be put to no better use than being spent in desire to parade with a white woman as his wife' (Gilmore, 1973)."*

The **Philadelphia Tribune's** headline put his situation more sardonically: *"Jack Johnson, dangerously ill, victim of white fever* (Jack Johnson, dangerously ill, victim of white fever, 1912).*"* Johnson's trial began on May 7, 1913. During court, the prosecution attempted to put Johnson's sexual proclivities on display in order to sway the jury. Whether it was to his detriment or to his benefit, he did not feign modesty, nor did he offer any sort of remorse. *"On the stand Johnson showed the most prized quality of the Bad Nigger—the ability to stand up to and outsmart white authority. In fact, for years any black who so challenged authority was dubbed 'Jack Johnson.' On the stand Johnson refused to be humiliated. He refused to lower his eyes and look humble. His gestures were those not of a contrite man who sought atonement but of one who believed he had done nothing wrong (Roberts, 1983)."*

Did Schreiber and he sometimes travel together? Yes. Did he know she was a prostitute? Yes. Did he ever pay for sex? No, he didn't have to: He was Jack Johnson! Had he ever given Schreiber any money? Yes, but not for sex. They were friends. He had once rented a flat and furniture for her sister and mother. If Schreiber called periodically and needed some financial help, he sent it. In fact, he had also once wired her money because Schreiber had gotten kicked out of the high-end brothel where she had worked due to her affiliation with him (yes, even prostitution had a color-line) and needed some help restarting.

It took five days of testimony to an all-white, all-male jury of 12 before the trial was over. When Johnson's guilty verdict was announced, his omnipresent smile slowly disappeared from his face. Sentencing took place on June 4, 1913. He faced a maximum punishment of five years, a $10,000 fine, or a combination of both. Despite the public and the prosecution wanting to make an example of him, Johnson was given a sentence of only one year and one day. Judge George Carpenter, who handed down the punishment, did not fully believe in the constitutionality of the Mann Act, and there is some evidence to suggest he did not fully believe Johnson was guilty. Nevertheless, the prosecution and, by extension, the American public, now had its pound of flesh. Johnson couldn't be beat in the ring, but the power structure had finally beaten him outside of it in court. Through it all, Johnson was as defiant as ever.

"As his lawyers filed for a new trial, the champion raced about the streets of Chicago in his expensive automobiles. On one of these cars he had installed a 'cut-out muffler,' which was noted for its noise. He made no attempts to conceal his movements, and even when fined he refused to adjust his muffler. Fast and loud was the pattern of his life, the source of his fame and troubles, and he saw no reason to alter his style as long as he was free (Roberts, 1983)." Johnson was given time to get his affairs in order before he reported to jail.

Railroaded in court and on top of the boxing world, he planned his escape. In his book, Johnson tells the tale of him fleeing the country by pretending to be a member of a Negro League baseball team. Supposedly, he made his exodus with them, into Canada, and then to England (Johnson J. , 2018). This part of his mythos was even put into the 1967 play, **The Great White Hope** (it won a Tony Award and a Pulitzer Prize in 1969), written by Howard Sackler, later made into the 1970 movie of the same name, which starred James Earl Jones in the title role (he received a Best Actor nomination for his portrayal).

Yet, as with everything, this is how Johnson wanted to be seen, not as things actually played out. There is strong evidence to suggest that some of the same government officials who prosecuted Johnson were the ones who accepted bribes from him to turn the other way as he left in self-exile. Johnson flipped the script and even admitted to as much years after the ordeal (Roberts, 1983). Regardless, the U.S. government did not seriously pursue Johnson after he fled the United States. It took on the attitude, *"Good Riddance!"*

Once in England, he was warmly received initially, but his arrogance quickly wore out his welcome and did not endear him to the public. English officials, who did not want to ruin their relationship with the United States, quietly asked him to leave. From there, Johnson bounced around Europe, attempting to make money through boxing, vaudeville shows, and even wrestling. However, the quality of boxers in Europe was not the same as those in the United States. Contests with European pugilists and Johnson were usually lackluster and tepid. Plus, the purses were far less lucrative. The other endeavors he got into garnered even less money and sometimes put him in dehumanizing positions. Johnson frequently backed out of participation in these events, or reneged on them after they started, because of disagreements with the operators of the business.

He was continuously sued and often lost more money than he made. Then, the unthinkable happened. On July 28, 1914, World War One began. This further hampered Johnson's economic viability. Boxing, and everything associated with it, instantly became a distant concern to those surrounded by rampant devastation and destruction. The shiny diamond Johnson once appeared to be was now a lackluster piece of cubic zirconia. With debts piling up and his ability to make money limited, he was running out of options. Then, one finally came to him: Defending his title against a legit boxer, albeit another Great White Hope from America, Jess Willard.

It came with a $30,000 guarantee and a third of the movie proceeds, which would make his portion even bigger; Johnson's opponent would get 25% of the gate receipts and a third of the movie proceeds as well (Jack Johnson vs. Jess

Willard, 2016). Willard, known as the *"Pottawatomie Giant,"* was one of boxing's anomalies and is one of its most interesting stories. The 6'6, 242lbs (some accounts say he was 235lbs, others that he was 245lbs) pugilist had the unheard arm reach of 83 inches. He did not begin his boxing career until he was 27 years old, but proved himself capable in the ring. In 1913, Willard had killed a boxer, Jack *"Bull"* Young, in a prizefight when he *"...punched Young so hard in the head that a piece of his broken jaw was driven into his skull and he died in the 9th round. While Willard was charged with second-degree murder, he fought the charges in court and won (Hoosevelt, 2020)."* Roberts (1983), who lists Willard as weighing in excess of 250lbs, was not impressed by him.

"As a boxer he was severely handicapped by poor defensive technique and slow hands and feet, but he was as good as, perhaps better than, most of the other White Hopes. After a checkered career that included more than a score of unimpressive victories and a few equally unimpressive defeats, he knocked out two fighters in quick succession. It was at that point he challenged Johnson, but rather than press his luck and ruin his modest string of victories, he withdrew from active boxing. This enraged other fighters whose managers proclaimed Willard 'no better qualified to fight for the title than the average spermaceti whale.' But the cessation had its merits, the most important of which was keeping Willard's stock with the public reasonably high (Roberts, 1983)."

The match between Willard and Johnson was arranged by Jack Curley, a promoter who had worked with Johnson before. Because of the war going on in Europe, it was decided the best location for the fight would be close to America, in Juarez, Mexico. Johnson left Europe in early 1915, headed for Havana, Cuba, where he would train for the fight. By then, revolution had broken out in Mexico and the country was fractured into pieces and individually controlled by revolutionaries. There were also rumors Johnson would be arrested and returned to the United States if he stepped onto Mexican soil. Venustiano Carranza, a toady for the revolutionary Alvaro Obregon, who had captured Mexico

City, later confirmed this (Roberts, 1983). Curley therefore switched the fight venue to Havana.

While Willard trained hard for the fight of his life, Johnson didn't appear to take things seriously. The documentary, **Unforgivable Blackness: The Rise and Fall of Jack Johnson**, discusses the fact that at this point in his life Johnson was 37 years old. There comes a time in all boxers' careers where they aren't as hungry as they used to be and lose the passion to fight like they once did (Barnes P. , Burns, & Schaye, 2004). Johnson was no exception. Taken into account all he had been through since being in exile, he was probably caught in the euphoria of being back in the limelight. Johnson had had his freedom in Europe, but had been unable to live the life he was accustomed to in America. Being in a familiar element might have encouraged him to become too relaxed. Roberts (1983) agrees with Ward's assessment of Johnson's pre-fight preparation for the Willard fight.

"For a boxer he was old; he turned thirty-seven on March 31, less than a week before he fought Willard. What he needed was about three months of hard work. What he settled for was a month of light workouts. Reporters watched him as he failed to complete his training sessions. He would set out for a 9-mile run and quit after 5 miles. Scheduled sparring sessions were postponed with alarming frequency. Mostly, Johnson posed—for stills, for moving pictures, for Cubans who had never before seen a boxing champion. It was as if he were a boxer in a side show— all he had to do to defeat the local yokels was look strong and mean (Roberts, 1983)." Willard was far from being a local yokel. He was not necessarily the real deal, but born three years after Johnson he was younger and perhaps stronger than anyone Johnson had ever fought.

Looking at it in a pragmatic sense, Willard wasn't a snack. A man had to be prepared to eat a full buffet of food if he stood before him. The Kansas cowboy had even said as much. Willard expected to take a beating for 10 or maybe 15 rounds and had trained to fight that way (Johns, 2020). The results of the contest, then, were perhaps predictable.

The fight took place at the Oriental Park Racetrack in Havana in front of approximately 20,000 people on April 5, 1915. The contest was scheduled for 45 rounds. Multitudes in the crowds had white flags in their hands to signify their racial preference for Willard. *"Guards armed with rifles and machetes surrounded the ring to make sure there was no trouble (Barnes P. , Burns, & Schaye, 2004)."* Tellingly, Johnson wasn't his usual exuberant self as he climbed into the ring. As the fight began, it appeared it would go the way all the other Great White Hope fights had gone.

Johnson dominated the fight from the start and was unusually aggressive in the beginning rounds. Predictably, Willard showed his lack of experience against him. *"While Willard did most of the leading in, Johnson did the majority of the scoring with hard punches and occasional headlong rushes. Despite the attacks from Johnson, Willard absorbs what Johnson dished out without showing any worse for wear (Johns, 2020)."* Johnson then began opening up even more in the ensuing rounds. *"The 12th saw Johnson unleash a furious burst that drove Willard to the ropes but, once again, the challenger shook off the damage and resumed his patient, jab-heavy boxing. The tenor of the fight began to turn in the 17th when Willard stepped up his forward movement as well as his work rate. Most of his one-twos fell short of the mark or were muffled by Johnson's open gloves but Willard's proactive attitude sent a forbidding message to the champion: "I am still strong and you still have nearly 30 more rounds of fighting to do (Jack Johnson vs. Jess Willard, 2016)."*

After throwing everything, except the kitchen sink at Willard, Johnson began to tire. By the 20th round, it was obvious to him that, while he might be the better boxer, Willard was in better shape. Johnson didn't have the stamina to beat him. Looking over at his wife in-between rounds, he knew what was coming soon and he didn't want her to see it. *"At the end of round twenty-five Johnson told Curley to take Lucille out of the arena. He was tired, he said, and could not last much longer (Roberts, 1983)."* Every great fighter comes to the end of the road; many of them get knocked out at some point in time. This was Johnson's time.

"The end came shortly before the halfway point of round 26. As the pair maneuvered toward the challenger's corner, Willard fired a lunging jab followed by a pulverizing right to the jaw. Upon impact, Johnson's head snapped violently to the side while his hands reached out and tried to take Willard down with him. That effort failed, so his stricken frame slid down Willard's torso and legs before landing back-first with a thud. As Johnson shaded his eyes from the blinding sun, referee Welsh positioned himself four feet directly behind the champion's head and tolled the count. Once he reached '10,' he immediately raised Willard's right arm and walked toward the ring center (Johns, 2020)."

If Willard and Johnson had fought in today's era, the fight wouldn't have lasted as long and Johnson would have won by unanimous decision. Today's professional boxing matches only go a maximum of twelve rounds and Johnson was well ahead on points (the death of boxer Kim Duk-koo in the ring by Ray *"Boom Boom"* Manchini on November 13, 1982, prompted the World Boxing Organization and many other pugilistic bodies to limit their contests to only 12 rounds). *"After the fight, referee Jack Welch said: 'If I had been compelled to give a decision at the end of the twenty-fifth round, it would have been Johnson's by a wide margin. Up to the twentieth round, Willard had only won one round by a real margin and two or three others by the slightest shade. In the thirteenth and fourteenth, I was almost sure Johnson would knock Willard out, but Willard showed that his jaw and body were too tough. Johnson put up a wonderful fight to the twentieth round, but age stepped in then and defeated him' (Jack Johnson vs. Jess Willard, 2016)."*

After the fight, Johnson showed humility by telling the **New York Times**, *"It was a clean knockout and the best man won. It was not a matter of luck. I have no kick coming (Jack Johnson vs. Jess Willard, 2016)."* Several months later, however, Johnson changed his tune. After being paid $250 by Nat Fleischer (future publisher of **The Ring Magazine**), he claimed to have received $50,000 and a promise that he would be able to return to the U.S. and avoid arrest if he threw the fight.

Of course, years after making this *"confession,"* Johnson *"confessed"* again, stating *"…he was in need of money and had said that no one would have wanted to purchase a statement that declared he had lost honestly. Fleischer said he bought the confession in order to suppress it since Johnson had already confirmed his story wasn't true. Willard was never implicated in the alleged fix (Jack Johnson vs. Jess Willard, 2016)."* When he heard this, Willard sarcastically replied, *"...if Johnson throwed it, I wish he throwed it sooner. It was hotter than hell down there (Jack Johnson vs. Jess Willard, 2016)."*

Johnson returned to England after the fight but, after the Englishmen saw that his arrogance had not changed—he became involved in a couple of lawsuits—he was again quietly asked to leave on February 29, 1916, by the Home Secretary, who gave him three days to vacate the country (Roberts, 1983). Unable to go to France because of the war, he went to Spain and lived there for several years, becoming involved in uneventful boxing matches to net some money. In 1919, Johnson left Spain and went to Mexico (different revolutionaries were now in control with a different set of politics), momentarily living rather comfortably there. He fell in favor with Venustiano Carranza's crowd, the Mexican revolutionary who had consolidated his power and controlled much of Mexico at that point of time.

Carranza was very anti-American so Johnson didn't have to worry about being extradited to the U.S. However, this passed when Carranza was assassinated in May 1920. Once again, the political climate suddenly changed. Estaban Cantu was now in power and Johnson was no longer favored. *"Cantu was looking for support both in Mexico and in the United States. Less than two weeks after Carranza was shot, Cantu told American agents that Johnson's standing in Mexico was no longer good. Indeed, the boxer had become involved in some 'crooked transactions,' and Cantu was anxious to deport him. If the United States would make a request, Cantu said, as a personal favor he would deliver Johnson to American authorities (Roberts, 1983)."*

Knowing it was only a matter of time before the walls closed in and tired of being in exile, Johnson made arrangements to turn himself in to U.S. authorities. Despite his continued efforts to con his way out of jail, he began serving his time on September 19, 1920, at the Leavenworth Prison in Leavenworth, Kansas; inmate number 15461. To Johnson's fortune, the Prison Superintendent, Denver S. Dickerson, was the ex-governor of Nevada who had allowed him to fight Jeffries in the Reno bout.

An avid fan of prizefighting, Dickerson made Johnson's stay in jail as comfortable as possible. He was made the Athletic Director of the prison and he put on several boxing exhibitions during his stay there. He was released on July 9, 1921. To say the United States had changed while Johnson had been away in exile and in prison would have been an understatement: The Red Summer of 1919 showed everyone that. Even boxing had undergone a major metamorphosis. Jack Dempsey was the new Heavyweight Champion and the war had altered America's perspective toward prizefighting. Pugilism was now more socially acceptable. It turns out unbridled aggression—barbarism—isn't all bad. The trait helped the Allies to win the war.

Johnson continued to box even when he was way past his prime. His last match, which ended in a loss to Walter Pierce, was in 1938. On June 10, 1946, Johnson and a friend named Fred Scott stopped at a local diner outside Raleigh, North Carolina. They were forced to eat in the back of the restaurant. Humiliated and incensed at being treated like a second-class citizen, the two finished their meals and Johnson angrily took the wheel, driving 70mph. Turning a curve on the highway, he crashed the car and both occupants were thrown from the vehicle. While Scott barely had a scratch on him, Johnson died in the hospital a couple of hours later (Barnes P. , Burns, & Schaye, 2004).

After Johnson lost the title in 1915, there wouldn't be another African American Heavyweight Champion for 22 years, when Joe Louis won the mantle on June 22, 1937. There would be a concerted effort by Louis' camp for Louis to be portrayed as squeaky clean, to counter the images of Johnson's past. Louis would come to resent Johnson, in part, because of pressure to keep up this façade (Roberts, 1983).

To the relief of many white Americans, Louis would be the antithesis of Johnson in terms of actions and demeanor. America wouldn't have to worry about another *"dangerous"* black man in the ring until Cassius Clay, the *"Louisville Lip,"* became Muhammad Ali. Speaking of Muhammad Ali…

There have been many comparisons between Johnson and Ali. Indeed, Ali saw much of himself in how Johnson was treated, but the two lauded boxers couldn't have been more different. Yes, they both had their share of legal problems with the government, but Ali stood his ground and fought the system. He did not flee to another country! Though hindsight is 20/20, had Johnson remained in the United States and served his time he would have been out in a year and been allowed to maximize his career potential, not banished in Europe during his prime, boxing has-beens, eking out a living.

Yes, both Ali and Johnson had their problems with white America, but since when has any black man—even one as accommodating as Booker T. Washington—ever been fully accepted? Additionally, the only time Johnson ever said anything remotely close to advancing the social cause of Blacks or gaining better Civil Rights was when he was in trouble with the law. Ali, on the other hand, never shirked his

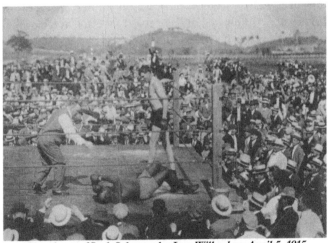

Knockout of Jack Johnson by Jess Willard on April 5, 1915

responsibility to Blacks or advancing their cause. His presence in that regard was almost omniscient. He gave up arguably the best years of his pugilistic career standing up for an idea.

This is one of the reasons many consider him the greatest boxer of all time, for the sacrifices he made inside AND outside the ring. While Johnson might be considered the best boxer of all time by some, his selfishness outside the ring makes him fall short of being a prizefighting great like Ali. Another thing that detracts from Johnson's greatness is his implementation of reverse racism.

Once he won the Heavyweight title, he refused to fight another African American boxer, thinking it was not good business (Roberts, 1983). While there is some truth to this— he stood to make more money in prizefights against white boxers because white Americans wanted him beat so badly— to commit such an egregious act against one's own race, especially when it was previously done by another, makes Johnson the ultimate hypocrite.

That being said, nothing can diminish what Johnson stood for, accomplished, and represented. He was a disruptor of the system, by any means necessary: His means. *"He wouldn't let anybody define him,"* says James Earl Jones in **Unforgiveable Blackness**. *"He was a self-defined man. And this issue of his being black was not that relevant to him. But the issue of his being free was very relevant (Barnes P. , Burns, & Schaye, 2004)."* It is said that great men are complex and, if nothing else, Johnson was as complex as it gets. Perhaps because he had grown up with white children in the ghettos of Galveston and had eaten in their households, Johnson didn't see himself any different than anyone White.

Indeed, maybe because he didn't recognize this difference, he didn't see himself as Black, either, only just a man and he lived his life as such: Not constrained by the limitations of the racial hierarchy and pseudo equality of the United States. Yes…perhaps. However, even Johnson had once admitted, *"I'm black. They'll never let me forget it. I'm black, all right! I'll never let them forget it! (Troutman, 2020)."* Maybe now that he's pardoned, America will stop seeing Johnson as *"dangerous"* and allow him to be viewed as he saw himself: Simply as a man. A pity that black males in America are unlikely to be allowed the same luxury.

Works Cited

Advice To Jack Johnson. (1910, July 14). *New York Age.*

Alderman, D. H., Inwood, J., & Tyner, J. A. (2018). Jack Johnson versus Jim Crow: Race, Reputation, and the Politics of Black Villainy: The Fight of the Century. *Southeastern Geographer, 58*(3), 227-249.

Barnes, P., Burns, K., Schaye, D. (Producers), Ward, G. C. (Writer), & Burns, K. (Director). (2004). *Unforgivable Blackness: The Rise and Fall of Jack Johnson* [Motion Picture]. PBS.

Basu, T. (2016, July 12). *inverse.com.* Retrieved August 12, 2020, from Why Americans See Black Men as a Threat: https://www.inverse.com/article/18159-science-of-racism-against-black-americans-police-shootings-research

Blakemore, E. (2019, July 24). *America Flirted with Legalized Prostitution During the Civil War.* Retrieved September 6, 2020, from history.com: America Flirted with Legalized Prostitution During the Civil War

Blassingame, J. (1975). Introduction. In A. Gilmore, *The National Impact of Jack Johnson* (pp. 3-8). New York: National University Publications.

Bressin, L. (n.d.). *Battle Royale: The Evolution of Exploitation.* Retrieved August 23, 2020, from longiewood.edu: http://www.longwood.edu/staff/miskecjm/446Bressin2.htm

Broome, R. (1979). The Australian Reaction to Jack Johnson, Black Pugilist, 1907-9. In R. Cashman, M. McKerman, R. Cashman, & M. McKerman (Eds.), *Sports History: The Making of Modern Sporting History* (pp. 344-45). St. Lucia, Australia: University of Queensland Press.

Burns, K. (2004, September). *The Women in Jack Johnson's Life*. Retrieved August 25, 2020, from pbs.org: https://www.pbs.org/kenburns/unforgivable-blackness/women#:~:text=Mary%20Austin&text=No%20record%20exists%20of%20this,but%20far%20from%20the%20last.

Burns, K. (2004). *Unforgiveable Blackness: Jack Johnson and the Law*. Retrieved September 6, 2020, from pbs.org: https://www.pbs.org/kenburns/unforgivable-blackness/johnsons-arrest

Cartwright, S. (n.d.). *In Debow's Review: "Diseases and Peculiarities of the Negro Race"*. Retrieved August 16, 2020, from pbs.org: https://www.pbs.org/wgbh/aia/part4/4h3106t.html

Champion Jack Johnson Denies Charges Against him in the Daily Newspapers. (1912, October 26). *Chicago Defender*, 1.

Christie, M. (n.d.). *On This Day: Jack Johnson dominates Tommy Burnsto win the world heavyweight title*. Retrieved August 31, 2020, from boxingnewsonline.net: https://www.boxingnewsonline.net/on-this-day-jack-johnson-dominates-tommy-burns-to-win-the-world-heavyweight-title/

Congress passes Mann Act aimed at curbing sex trafficking. (2020, June 23). Retrieved September 6, 2020, from history.com: https://www.history.com/this-day-in-history/congress-passes-mann-act

Davis, A. J., Stevenson, B., Western, B., Mauer, M., & Travis, J. (2018). *Policing the Black Man: Arrest, Prosecution, and Imprisonment*. (A. J. Davis, Ed.) New York, New York: Vintage Books.

Domonoske, C. (2018, May 24). *Legendary Boxer Jack Johnson Gets Pardon, 105 Years After Baseless Conviction.* Retrieved September 3, 2020, from npr.org: https://www.npr.org/sections/thetwo-way/2018/05/24/614114966/legendary-boxer-jack-johnson-gets-pardon-105-years-after-baseless-conviction

Donaldson, L. (2015, August 12). *theguardians.com.* Retrieved August 12, 202, from When the media misrepresents black men, the effects are felt in the real world: https://www.theguardian.com/commentisfree/2015/aug/12/media-misrepresents-black-men-effects-felt-real-world

DuBois, W. (1914, August). The Prize Fighter. *The Crisis, 8*(4), 181.

Ebert, R. (1975, July 5). *Reviews: Mandingo.* Retrieved August 13, 2020, from robertebert.com: https://www.rogerebert.com/reviews/mandingo-1975

Edwards, F., Esposito, M., & Lee, H. (2019, August 5). *pnas.org.* Retrieved August 10, 2020, from Risk of being killed by police use of force in the United States by age, race–ethnicity, and sex: https://www.pnas.org/content/116/34/16793

Eligon, J., & Thorpe, B. K. (2018, May 24). *Missed in Coverage of Jack Johnson, the Racism Around Him.* Retrieved August 25, 2020, from newyorktimes.com: https://www.nytimes.com/2018/05/24/sports/jack-johnson-racism.html

Fetter, H. (July, 2010 3). *The Fight of the Century -- Really.* Retrieved September 3, 2020, from theatlantic.com: https://www.theatlantic.com/entertainment/archive/2010/07/the-fight-of-the-century-really/59134/

Franco, R. J. (2016, November 21). *Sparring in the White House: Theodore Roosevelt, Race, and Boxing*. Retrieved August 23, 2020, from ussporthistory.com: Sparring in the White House: Theodore Roosevelt, Race, and Boxing

Franco, R. J. (2017, November 22). *The Thanksgiving an imprisoned Jack Johnson fought two men at Leavenworth*. Retrieved September 7, 2020, from theundefeated.com: https://theundefeated.com/features/the-thanksgiving-an-imprisoned-jack-johnson-fought-two-men-at-leavenworth/

Garcia, R. (2019, December 26). *Dec. 26, 1908: Burns vs Johnson*. Retrieved August 31, 2020, from thefightcity.com: https://www.thefightcity.com/dec-26-1908-burns-vs-johnson-boxing/

George Dixon. (2020, July 25). Retrieved August 23, 2020, from britannica.com: https://www.britannica.com/biography/George-Dixon-boxer

Gilmore, A.-T. (1975). *Bad Nigger! The National Impact of Jack Johnson*. Port Washington, New York: National University Publications.

Gilmore, A.-T. (1973). Jack Johnson and White Women: The National Impact. *Journal of Negro History, 58*(1), 18-38.

Gilmore, A.-T. (1995). Black Athletes In An Historical Context: The Issue of Race. *Negro History Bulletin, 58*(3/4), 7-14.

Green, L. (n.d.). *Negative Racial Stereotypes and Their Effect on Attitudes Toward African-Americans*. Retrieved August 12, 2020, from feris.edu: https://www.ferris.edu/htmls/news/jimcrow/links/essays/vcu.htm

Grossman, R. (2018, May 24). *Commentary: Jack Johnson —
pardoned by Trump — fought hard against racism.*
Retrieved September 5, 2020, from latimes.com:
https://www.latimes.com/nation/ct-perspec-flash-
jack-johnson-trial-mann-act-0527-20180523-
story.html

Hoosevelt, T. (2020, March 14). *Jack Dempsey Vs. Jess Willard
1919: The Most Brutal Fight In History.* Retrieved
September 7, 2020, from Historythings.com:
https://historythings.com/jack-dempsey-vs-jess-
willard-1919-brutal-fight-history/

Husband, S. (2016, May). *BOLD, BRASH AND PROUD:
JACK JOHNSON.* Retrieved August 31, 2020, from
therake.com:
https://therake.com/stories/icons/jack-johnson/

Jack Johnson. (n.d.). Retrieved August 25, 2020, from
myblackhistory.net:
http://www.myblackhistory.net/Jack_Johnson.htm

Jack Johnson vs. Jess Willard. (2016, May 27). Retrieved
September 7, 2020, from boxrec.com:
https://boxrec.com/media/index.php/Jack_Johnso
n_vs._Jess_Willard

Jack Johnson, dangerously ill, victim of white fever. (1912,
October 26). *Philadelphia Tribune*, 7.

James J. Jefferies. (n.d.). Retrieved August 29, 2020, from
boxrec.com:
https://boxrec.com/media/index.php/James_J._Jef
fries

Jefferson, T. (n.d.). *Notes on the State of Virginia: Electronic
Version.* Retrieved August 16, 2020, from
docsouth.unc.edu:
https://docsouth.unc.edu/southlit/jefferson/jeffers
on.html

Johns, M. (2020, April 5). *Jess Willard knocks out Jack Johnson*. Retrieved September 7, 2020, from bigfightweekend.com: https://bigfightweekend.com/history/jess-willard-knocks-out-jack-johnson/

Johnson, C. J. (2018, May 25). *The short, sad story of Cafe de Champion — Jack Johnson's mixed-race nightclub on Chicago's South Side*. Retrieved September 1, 2020, from chicagotribune.com: https://www.chicagotribune.com/history/ct-met-cafe-de-champion-jack-johnson-chicago-20180525-story.html

Johnson, J. (2018). *My Life In The Ring & Out* (Vol. 1). Meneola: Dover Publications, Incorporated.

London, J. (1908, December 27). Jack London Describes the Fight and Jack Johnson's Golden Smile. *New York Herald*, 1.

Loubriel, J. (2016, July 10). *4 Racist Stereotypes White Patriarchy Invented to 'Protect' White Womanhood*. Retrieved August 13, 2020, from everydayfeminism.com: https://everydayfeminism.com/2016/07/protect-white-womanhood/

Lussana, S. (2010). To See Who Was Best on the Plantation: Enslaved Fighting Contests and Masculinity in the Antebellum Plantation South. *The Journal of Southern History, 76*(4), 901-922.

Markel, D. (2018, February 6). *The false, racist theory of eugenics once ruled science. Let's never let that happen again*. Retrieved August 16, 2020, from pbs.org: https://www.pbs.org/newshour/nation/column-the-false-racist-theory-of-eugenics-once-ruled-science-lets-never-let-that-happen-again

Marshall, M. (2020, June 24). *newsscientest.com.* Retrieved August 11, 2020, from US police kill up to 6 times more black people than white people Read more: https://www.newscientist.com/article/2246987-us-police-kill-up-to-6-times-more-black-people-than-white-people/#ixzz6Us5bBxW1:

McCormick, E. (2020, July 4). *July 4, 1910: Johnson vs Jeffries.* Retrieved September 1, 2020, from thefightcity.com: https://www.thefightcity.com/july-4-1910-johnson-vs-jeffries-jack-johnson-james-jeffries-corbett-sullivan-tommy-burns-fight-of-the-century/

McNeill, M. (2017, May 5). *A Brief History of Prostitution in the US.* Retrieved September 5, 2020, from libitarianinstitute.org: https://libertarianinstitute.org/articles/brief-history-prostitution-us/

Negro Enthusiast Killed. (1910, July 5). *The Democratic Banner, 53,* p. 1. Retrieved from https://chroniclingamerica.loc.gov/lccn/sn88078751/1910-07-05/ed-1/seq-1/#date1=1910&index=1&rows=20&words=Jack+Johnson+RIOT&searchType=basic&sequence=0&state=&date2=1910&proxtext=Jack+Johnson+Riot&y=22&x=8&dateFilterType=yearRange&page=1

Parthun, N. (2009, November). *Unforgivable Blackness: The Lingering Legacy of Jack Johnson.* Retrieved September 3, 2020, from publici.ucimc.org: http://publici.ucimc.org/2009/11/unforgivable-blackness-the-lingering-legacy-of-jack-johnson/

Philadelphia Inquirer. (1905, June 27). p. 10.

Pickens, W. (1910, July 30). Talladega College Professor Speaks on Reno Fight. *Chicago Defender,* 1.

Pilgrim, D. (2012, November). *The Brute Caricature*. Retrieved August 13, 2020, from ferris.edu: https://www.ferris.edu/jimcrow/brute/

Popular and Pervasive Stereotypes of African Americans. (n.d.). Retrieved August 13, 2020 , from nmaahc.com: https://nmaahc.si.edu/blog-post/popular-and-pervasive-stereotypes-african-americans

Race, the Power of Illusion: Go Deeper Timeline. (n.d.). Retrieved August 16, 2020, from pbs.org: https://www.pbs.org/race/000_About/002_03_d-godeeper.htm

Racism Takes a Blow in Reno. (n.d.). Retrieved September 1, 2020, from ibhof.com: http://www.ibhof.com/pages/archives/johnsonjeffries.html

Riemann, M. (2017, May 23). *When a black fighter won 'the fight of the century,' race riots erupted across America*. Retrieved September 3, 2020, from timeline.com: https://timeline.com/when-a-black-fighter-won-the-fight-of-the-century-race-riots-erupted-across-america-3730b8bf9c98

Roberts, J. B., & Skutt, A. G. (2006). *The Boxing Register: International Boxing Hall of Fame Official Record Book*. Ithaca, NY: McBooks Press.

Roberts, R. (1983). Galveston's Jack Johnson: Flourishing in the Dark. *The Southwestern Historical Quarterly, 87*(1), 37-56.

Roberts, R. (1983). *Papa Jack: Jack Johnson and the Era of White Hopes*. New York, New York: The Free Press.

Roosevelt Condemns Fight. (1910, July 14). Retrieved from newspapers.com: https://www.newspapers.com/clip/14924297/theodore-roosevelt-condemns-showing/

Ruane, M. E. (2019, April 30). *A brief history of the enduring phony science that perpetuates white supremacy*. Retrieved August 16, 2020, from washingtonpost.com: https://www.washingtonpost.com/local/a-brief-history-of-the-enduring-phony-science-that-perpetuates-white-supremacy/2019/04/29/20e6aef0-5aeb-11e9-a00e-050dc7b82693_story.html

Sad Crowd at Ringside. (1910, July 5). *New York Times*, p. 2.

Slack, J. (2015, February 3). *The War on Jack Johnson: Boxing's First Black Heavyweight Champion Versus the World*. Retrieved August 25, 2020, from vice.com: https://www.vice.com/en_us/article/9a4xxe/the-war-on-jack-johnson-boxings-first-black-heavyweight-champion-versus-the-world

Sommers, D. (1966). *The Rise of Sports in New Orleans 1850 - 1900*. Baton Rogue, LA: Louisiana State University Press.

Streible, D. (1989). A History of the Boxing Film, 1894-1915: Social Control and Social Reform in the Progressive Era. *Film History*(3), pp. 235-257.

Taylor, E., Guy, P.-W., & Wilke, P. (2019, May 7). The Historical Perspectives of Stereotypes on African-American Males. *Journal of Human Rights and Social Work*(4), 213-225. Retrieved from link.springer.com: https://link.springer.com/content/pdf/10.1007/s41134-019-00096-y.pdf

The Coon Caricature. (n.d.). Retrieved August 12, 2020, from ferris.edu: https://www.ferris.edu/jimcrow/coon/

Thomsen, I. (2020, July 16). *news.northeastern.edu*. Retrieved August 10, 2020, from THE RESEARCH IS CLEAR: WHITE PEOPLE ARE NOT MORE LIKELY THAN BLACK PEOPLE TO BE KILLED BY POLICE.: https://news.northeastern.edu/2020/07/16/the-research-is-clear-white-people-are-not-more-likely-than-black-people-to-be-killed-by-police/

Tommy Burns vs. Jack Johnson. (2017, November 24). Retrieved August 31, 2020, from boxrec.com: https://boxrec.com/media/index.php/Tommy_Burns_vs._Jack_Johnson

Trista. (n.d.). *An Exploration into Why the Word 'Hooker' Came to Describe Sex Workers.* Retrieved September 6, 2020, from historycollection.com: https://historycollection.com/an-exploration-into-why-the-word-hooker-came-to-describe-certain-workers/

Troutman, B. (2020, August 16). *Boxer Jack Johnson was an unapologetic, heroic trendsetter.* Retrieved September 7, 2020, from hillsdale.net: https://www.hillsdale.net/sports/20200816/boxer-jack-johnson-was-unapologetic-heroic-trendsetter

Two champs meet. (2005, January 17). Retrieved September 7, 2020, from U.S. News and World Report: https://web.archive.org/web/20131111070334/http://www.usnews.com/usnews/news/articles/050117/17burns.peo.htm

Vogan, T. (2010). Irrational Power: Jack Johnson, Przefighting Films, and Documentary Affect. *Journal of Sport History*, 397-413.

Walker, R. (2017, December 27). *The day Jack Johnson became the first black world heavyweight champion.* Retrieved August 31, 2020, from theundefeated.com: https://theundefeated.com/features/the-day-jack-johnson-became-the-first-black-world-heavyweight-champion/

Ward, G. C. (2004). *Unforgivable Blackness: The Rise and Fall of Jack Johnson.* New York: A.A. Knopf.

Washington, B. T. (1912, October 26). The National Impact Of Jack Johnson. *Baltimore Afro-American Ledger.*

Weinreb, M. (2016, June 13). *Before Ali, There Was Jack Johnson's Unforgivable Blackness*. Retrieved August 23, 2020, from vice.com: https://www.vice.com/en_uk/article/9apbja/throw back-thursday-before-ali-there-was-jack-johnson39s-unforgivable-blackness-uk-translation

Wilson, J. (2017, March 13). *Apa.org*. Retrieved August 10, 2020, from Date created: March 13, 2017 People See Black Men as Larger, More Threatening Than Same-Sized White Men: https://www.apa.org/news/press/releases/2017/03/black-men-threatening

Wine Flows Like Lapaloma Melody. (1912, July 12). Retrieved September 8, 2020, from The San Francisco Call: newspapers.com

Made in the USA
Coppell, TX
19 October 2020

39963174R00046